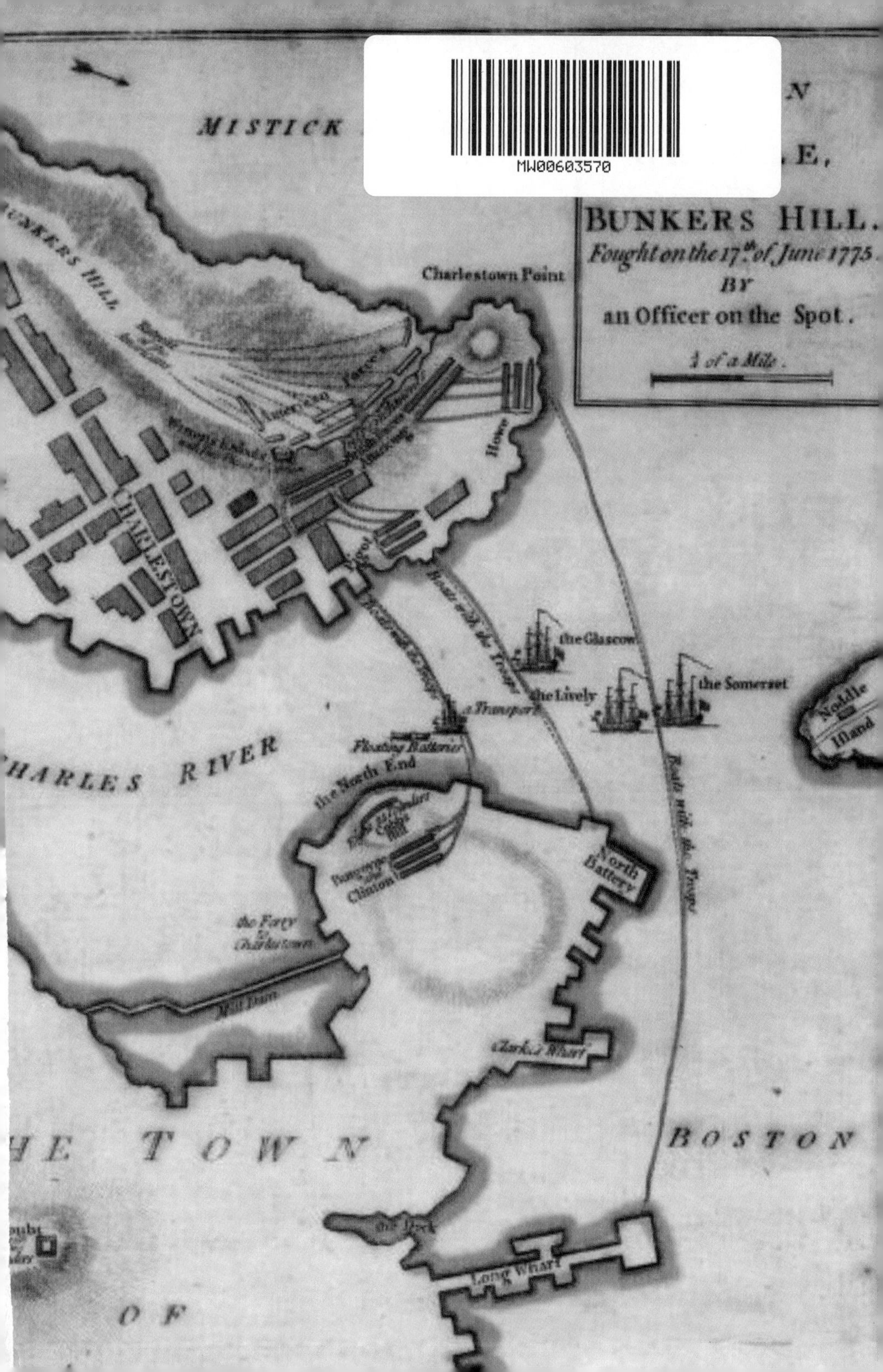

MW00603570
MISTICK
N
E,
BUNKERS HILL.
Fought on the 17th of June 1775.
BY
an Officer on the Spot.
¼ of a Mile.
Charlestown Point
Howe
CHARLESTOWN
the Glascow
the Lively
the Somerset
a Transport
Floating Batteries
CHARLES RIVER
the North End
Noddle Island
North Battery
Burgoyne and Clinton
the Ferry to Charlestown
Mill Dam
Clarke's Wharf
THE TOWN
BOSTON
OF
Long Wharf

The 18th-Century Woman

Women's issues in western civilization have been calling for reform long before the suffragette and women's liberation movements of the 19th and 20th centuries. Since before our nation existed ladies have spoken out in their personal letters and other writings about the need for educational equality and the restructuring of the laws concerning the legal ownership of their own properties and inheritances. During the Revolutionary era there were no feminine protest marches or demonstrations and arrests for speaking out on these topics, but make no mistake – these ladies set the tone for what was to come over the next 240+ years. And let's not forget that many women of this time were socially excluded from the entire discussion. Women of lesser fortunes, or no fortunes at all, were more concerned with feeding hungry children rather than whether they could debate classical literature or philosophy at a dinner party. Legally retaining property left by husbands or fathers meant little to women who were enslaved. And what of those whose land had been taken "legally" when tribal leaders signed treaties that they didn't fully understand. When reviewed only on the surface, 18th-century women's issues appear to revolve primarily around the concerns of women who came from more affluent backgrounds. But it's not that other women weren't significant, it's simply that more writings of women from wealthier families have survived. We can

WHICH CAME FIRST?

We've all heard the story of Betsy Ross and the making of the first American flag. We've all seen this flag in every movie about the American Revolution as it's waved valiantly in our struggle for freedom. What few people realize is that it was not the first American flag. Betsy Ross was asked to make her famous flag in May 1776. But six months earlier, in late 1775, a young widow named Rebecca Flower Young produced the first American flag, now known as the Grand Union Flag. The use of the British "Union Jack" rather than a circle of 13 stars made perfect sense in 1775, because the colonies had yet to declare any intentions for independence. We were still very much British!

read of their complaints, wants, and needs throughout their letters, poems, and even plays, which give us better insight to their particular frustrations and concerns. But there were many more concerns for women of less fortunate stations in society, and there were many more women in these circumstances. Our goal in this study is to utilize the details that we know from such women as Abigail Adams, Mercy Otis Warren, or Phillis Wheatley to bring to life the stories of other women – great women who simply aren't as well-known because they were neither rich, nor related to a founding father.

COVERTURE: All women in British society, in which American colonists were deeply embedded, were legally shackled to the cultural burdens of the laws of Coverture. Rooted in the French word *covert*, which means *to cover*, English laws of Coverture in the 18th century meant that women were legally "covered" by the protection of their husbands or fathers. Proponents of the law would argue that Coverture was designed to protect women from making foolish decisions that would cause them to lose their possessions and/or inheritances. Women, on the other hand, weren't so easily fooled, especially those who had the most to lose. Women who had inherited lands and other holdings from their fathers or deceased husbands found themselves in the fight of their lives when it came to marriage and/or remarriage. English laws sought to separate these ladies from their personal fortunes and bestow those treasures to their new husbands (can you tell that it was men who made these laws?). For men, Coverture provided a very simple and convenient process by which they became the legal and sole owners of whatever their wives brought into the marriage.

OUR ONEIDA ALLIES

One of the most neglected legacies of the American Revolution is the alliance of the Oneida Indians with those in rebellion. Most of the Native American tribes and confederacies chose to either rely upon their more stable relationships with Great Britain or simply wait to see the outcome of the war. The Oneida, however, became strong allies - playing a significant role in many battles, including the American victories at Fort Stanwyx and Saratoga. But perhaps the greatest example of the alliance between the Oneida and the American rebels took place during that historic winter at Valley Forge in 1777 - 1778. Under a directive from their chief, Oskanondonha, a party of Oneidas walked over 400 miles from their lands in New York to Valley Forge to bring corn to Washington's army. But when they returned home one Oneida woman, known as Polly Cooper, stayed behind to help feed the army and teach them the best ways to prepare the corn under such dire conditions. Tradition has it that when the Oneida woman wouldn't accept any pay, Washington offered her a shawl, which has become a symbol of Oneida honor. This statue depicting the images of Polly Cooper, Oskanondonha, and George Washington can be found in the National Museum of the American Indian (Smithsonian Institute) in Washington, D.C.

This gave the notion of men "marrying into money" a whole new meaning. But for women there was nothing simple nor convenient about it. A woman's ancestral lands could be sold for no other reason than her new husband so desired. If her husband had debts or needed funds for a risky investment or foolish venture, he would be well within his rights to put his wife's properties at risk rather than his own. Even poor farm women faced the same hazard. If a deceased husband had held his farm free and clear and the widow were to remarry, she would forfeit her land to her new husband and hope that his intentions were honest. Remember, this was a day and age when currency and baubles were extremely vulnerable to the economics of imperial policies and global politics. Land was the only truly solid investment, which is why the rich of this era were referred to as "landed gentry." As long as taxes on the land could be paid, farms and plantations – city homes and lots – guaranteed financial security. Fear of the laws of Coverture was so strong among 18th-century women that some sought resourceful solutions that were way ahead of their time. Kitty Greene, the widow of Revolutionary War hero General Nathanial Greene, found new love after her husband died but refused to marry. Rather than putting her lands at risk, Kitty and her beau lived together without the legal or religious sanctions of marriage. Polite society was so shocked by her actions that George Washington invited them to visit him at Mt. Vernon where the proper marriage services might be conducted. Washington even hinted in his letter of invitation that her life choices might easily be the reason that Congress had delayed granting her requests for the military pension that she was legally entitled for her late husband's service to the nation. But Kitty fully understood that to forfeit her property to a new husband was to forfeit her independence as an individual. If the ladies had learned

KITTY GREENE AND THE COTTON GIN

In 1792, Kitty Greene hired a young Yale graduate by the name of Eli Whitney to tutor her many children. It was while under her employ that Whitney invented the Cotton Gin. This crank-driven device revolutionized the process of removing cotton seeds from the raw product by hand to combing metal tines through the fiber to claw out the seeds. Many believe that it was Kitty Greene's suggestions that led this bright, young New Englander to find a faster, more efficient way to produce a refined product from this traditional southern crop.

nothing else from the Revolutionary experiences all around them, they learned a yearning for independence.

But not all women in the various colonial-era cultures were strangled by such issues. Native Americans believed that it was the Europeans who behaved like "savages" and said so quite often. One can't deny that European culture would not have survived in North America without the help of those same native people who would eventually be driven to near extinction. But of all the things that Europeans learned from the Indians, how to treat women was not among them. Cherokee society of the Revolutionary era, for example, embraced a culture of matrilineal kinship. Simply put, a person's heritage was traced through their mother's family; sons took their mothers' family names. And since the Cherokee built their homes around the tradition of the extended family, great-grandmothers down to granddaughters –and their families – lived in close proximity to each other, if not in the same home. Husbands and sons shared these homes with their wives and grandmothers, etc., but since all of the dwellings in Cherokee towns belonged to the women, if there was a breakup in the marriage the husband would return to his own mother's home. Cherokee women worked the land and prepared the food for winter storage; they tanned deerskins for trade. Their role in the family and economy of the community was crucial to the tribe, both for survival as well as successful trade. Cherokee women, therefore, had equal rights to men in political discussions involving every aspect of Cherokee life – including war. In fact, if the circumstances dictated, some women would fight alongside the men in battle. These "War Women," as they were known among the Cherokee people, were heralded as heroes and noted

LEGEND OF THE GHIGAU

Women were highly respected in the Cherokee culture, but the role of Ghigau, or Beloved Woman, was the highest stature that a woman could achieve. In addition to the many rights and privileges bestowed to Cherokee women, a Ghigau had a vote in the General Council, a leadership role in the Women's Counci, and she prepared and served the ceremonial Black Drink (a purifier to cleanse one of physical and spiritual contamination). Ghigau also served as peace negotiators and could grant reprieve to prisoners condemned to die. The title of Ghigau also translated "War Woman." During the American Revolution a Cherokee woman by the name of Cuhtahlatah won the title of Ghigau by leading warriors to victory after her husband was killed earlier in battle.

1591 Engraving of Black Drink ceremony by Theodor De Bry

SALLY HEMINGS

By now, most have heard about Thomas Jefferson's improper relationship with one of his enslaved females, Sally Hemings. Sally, a house servant, bore six children to Jefferson, all of whom were raised to become Jefferson's house servants. But that's not the most disturbing factor in this historic dalliance. Sally Hemings was the child of John Wayles, Jefferson's father-in-law, and Betty Hemings, one of Wayles's house servants. They too had six children together, Sally being the youngest. Betty Hemings was the child of an English sea captain named Hemings and a "full-blooded African" woman who was owned by Francis Eppes - John Wayles's other son-in-law. Jefferson's oldest grandson, Thomas Jefferson Randolph, once stated that "A gentleman dining with Mr. Jefferson looked so startled as he raised his eyes from [Jefferson] to the servant behind him, that his discovery of the resemblance was perfectly obvious to all."

Sadly, this type of behavior wasn't uncommon in the Revolutionary era. Relationships such as this gave slave owners an additional sense of power over those that they owned, as they demonstrated in the most horrible way possible that they could take whatever they chose, from whomever they chose, in whatever manner they chose, and there was nothing anyone could do about it. It was not only a way to show their power over women, but it also let the enslaved men on the plantation know just how helpless they were to protect the women that they cared for. How many more African and African-American women suffered the indignities of Sally Hemings, we most likely will never know. We have no portraits of these women or tangible mementos, other than the comments and records kept by those who abused them.

for their bravery among the tribes and nations.

In British culture, divorce was rarely an option for colonial-era women, even when the laws were so conflicted and inconsistent that some cases were never settled properly. For example, divorce wasn't allowed in England; however, it was permitted in several of the American colonies. This made for an extremely messy situation when lawful colonial divorces were re-filed and overturned by an English court. If a woman were to obtain a legal divorce in the colonies, remarry, then have her divorce reversed in London, what was her social status to be? And what if a child was born to the new couple in the meantime? This was an era when a woman's reputation and a child's paternity was the difference between social acceptance and public shunning – and neither were to be taken lightly.

The 18th-century woman had many concerns and restrictions, the likes of which we today can't imagine. And yet one British officer serving under General Charles Lord Cornwallis made the comment, "We may destroy all the men in America and we shall still have all we can do to defeat the women." These women were some of the most adamant and faithful followers – and leaders, in their own way – for the cause of independence from 1775 to 1783. And other women were equally as loyal to King George III, no matter the cost. In either case, these women were rarely what we imagine the "typical" woman of the colonial age to be, for there were many more Molly Pitchers than Betsy Rosses.

The Home Front

Whether the men were underfoot, away at war, on hunting trips, or presiding over the birth of a new nation, it was always the women's duty to keep the home intact. But, for what it was worth, at least in the home women had a say. Here, they knew more about what was going on than the men. Here, their decisions were important. In the home they were in charge of running the activities of the house, attending to the needs of sick family members, keeping household supplies, food, and drink properly and sufficiently stored, and seeing that servants (if they had them) were hard at work. In the home the women were generals, though open recognition of this status was more understood than stated. Even with as much credit and respect as John Adams gave to his wife Abigail – even with as much as he depended upon her business sense and intuition to keep their estate from bankruptcy – she could still be over-ridden on any issue in the home if he so chose.

The more prominent a woman's station in society, the busier they were in the home. In some homes, parties, dinners, dances, and balls were expected to be elaborately thrown and often. Those who could afford fine silver, crystal, linens, and china were expected to oversee the proper care and storage of these precious commodities so that they were readily available for use and/or inspection. Many Southern women entertained at their plantations in order to drive away boredom during those times of the year when their husbands' presence was required at rural properties. To invite guests so far from town meant that they most likely would spend the night – perhaps several nights. As a result, bedrooms had to be properly prepared and impressively laundered. Ministers' wives who might have no staff or servants were still expected to be prepared for groups of church members or visiting clergymen, often on short notice. When protests shaped into the Non-Consumption/ Non-Importation boycotts, colonial leaders placed the success of these efforts

Non-Consumption/ Non-Importation Boycotts

As early as 1766, colonial leaders agreed to boycott items that they felt were unjustly taxed, such as legal documents, newspapers, pamphlets, licenses - even playing cards and wax. Events grew worse in 1767, with new taxes on glass, lead, paint, paper, and tea. By the end of 1768 there were great efforts to boycott the consumption and importation of many British goods, above all those that could be made in the colonies. In 1774, the non-consumption/non-importation boycotts were re-born and expanded to include any goods coming from Britain or being sold to English merchants. Violators of the agreements found their names published in colonial newspapers, their shops and homes vandalized, and often faced physical harm.

THE EDENTON TEA PARTY

On March 20, 1775, Penelope Barker of North Carolina organized what became known as the "Edenton Tea Party." Penelope found 51 ladies from her town who would commit to the non-consumption/non-importation of British goods by signing a declaration of support for the boycott. When news of their written protest reached London the ladies were ridiculed as foolish, for what importance could women have on political and economic events? A cartoon of the gathering was circulated in British papers hoping to make the ladies of Edenton look ridiculous. What they weren't taking into consideration was that the boycotts couldn't succeed without the women to hand-make clothes and refuse to purchase the goods necessary to keep the home life bearable - goods that quite often were either created by the labor of women or utilized by women in the home.

Notice how the drawing mocks these women by showing an unattended child being licked by a dog

directly on the women. It was they who had to completely re-direct their everyday routines and convert the home into a small factory or "cottage industry."

Martha Washington, for example, was known to be with her husband during the harsh winter months in Cambridge, Valley Forge, Morristown, and Newburgh. At night there were often dances and dinners, which Martha enjoyed greatly, but her primary concern was her husband's troops. In the daylight hours Martha was steadily about her duties to the cause of independence, in particular being what she called a "pattern of industry" – a good example for other ladies to follow – concerning the boycotts. One woman recounted the time that she and other well-placed ladies of Morristown called on Martha. They came in their finest silks and gowns, only to find Mrs. Washington in a simple dress and apron, knitting socks for herself and her husband. Martha politely reminded them that "the separation from the mother country will dry up the resources whence many of our comforts are derived. We must become independent by our determination to do without what we cannot make ourselves. Whilst our husbands and brothers are examples of patriotism we must be patterns of industry."

THE "KEY" TO HAPPINESS

Keys were symbols of the security of the home, both in its safekeeping and its finances. It's not unusual to find a key etched on the grave stones of women, signifying that she was the possessor of the key and, therefore, the authority within its walls - at least if the man was smart, she was!

Young girls of every level of society were often sent away to be trained in, and to perfect, the art of properly running a house, cooking, sewing, spinning cloth, child care, the instruction of servants, etc. For girls, education and the proper running of the home were one and the same. One minister's wife in Rhode Island had no children of her own to depend upon for running a very busy home and she couldn't find local girls to help. She was soon overjoyed by the arrival of a teenage girl from Philadelphia, whose father was a judge and prominent attorney. The girl's younger sister, by the way, was Peggy Shippen who would later become the wife of Benedict Arnold.

SOUTHERN COMFORT

As the British began their drive from Charleston to Yorktown in 1780 and 1781, many rebel refugees fled in a northwestern direction toward present-day Charlotte, NC, always with the British juggernaut on their tail. There, they would find refuge and comfort at the home of John and Ann Barnett before continuing their journey to safety. The Barnett's might feed as many as fifty people a day and then have a retreating rebel army come down the road looking for provisions. One young straggler was a skinny boy in his early teens and his mother - both near starving, but too proud to admit it. The boy's name was Andrew Jackson.

Understanding the trauma of childbirth was critical to a young girl's training. So many women died during what was supposed to be such a blessed event that older daughters were often thrown into the role of mid-wife and physician to their mothers, and then

MOURNING WARS

Since the 1600s, settlers
blished "Captivity Narratives"
tories of family members
tured due to the Native
nerican practice of "replacing"
ceased loved ones with someone
om another tribe or settlement.
ary Jemison, was the victim of
"Mourning War" in 1758 when,
a teen, she was taken in a
d by French soldiers and their
awnee allies. Mary was then
aded to two Seneca women as
peace offering for the brother
ey lost in battle. Mary was
named Dehgewanus and wed
a Delaware warrior before moving to a Seneca village in western New York. Adoptees, such as Mary, saw the American Revolution from completely unique perspectives. Even when given the opportunity to return to white settlements, many of these people chose to remain with their newly adopted families and cultures. Many others who returned often regretted that decision and went back to their adopted villages. For Dehgewanus this decision was made easy when in 1779, George Washington ordered her village destroyed as a means to squash Iroquois support for the British.

A
NARRATIVE
OF THE
CAPTIVITY
AND
SUFFERINGS
OF
BENJAMIN GILBERT
AND HIS
FAMILY;
WHO WERE SURPRISED BY THE INDIANS, AND TAKEN FROM THEIR FARMS, ON THE FRONTIERS OF PENNSYLVANIA.
IN THE SPRING, 1780.
PHILADELPHIA, PRINTED:
LONDON:
Reprinted and Sold by JAMES PHILLIPS, George Yard, Lombard-street.
M. DCC. XC.

grief counselors to the other children in the home. Their role then was to become a surrogate mother with but a moment's notice. Nor was it uncommon for the mother to survive, but not the child. While John Adams was away at Congress, his wife Abigail lost a baby in childbirth. Yet even in the midst of her sorrow she writes how she thanked God to have survived to care for her other five children. For women who did survive childbirth it wasn't uncommon for them to have a child every couple of years, as long as they were physically able. In many cases, young mothers were called upon to assist in the birth and post-natal care of their own siblings. Margaret Morris and her husband, for example, took on her six younger siblings when her parents died in 1760 and 1761. Margaret was only 16 years old.

In the southern colonies, many women faced a completely different version of "running a house." All of the colonies south of the Chesapeake Bay, with the exception of East and West Florida, had fallen to the rebellion by September 1775 (technically, the royal governor of Georgia stayed-on as an obnoxious "advisor" until January, 1776). Loyalist men were faced with either signing a letter of oath to the rebellion or facing physical retribution, such as tar-and-feathering. As a result, a great number of these men fled to East and West Florida to escape their tormentors rather than recant their loyalty to king and country.

Some had bounties placed on their heads like common outlaws, while others were threatened with execution. But while fleeing to the Floridas made perfect sense for these men, they stranded their wives, families, and slaves in the occupied areas for the purpose of protecting their property. It was generally understood that if homes and property were occupied, whether located in a town or out in the rural regions – whether the property in question was a house, land, livestock, or enslaved human beings – that a common sense of honor kept everything secure. This seemed like a reasonable action at the time, regardless how cowardly we might view it today. But fighting in the southern backcountry was anything but civilized. These women and children lived under a constant cloud of danger, while slaves were vulnerable to capture or worse. Life became about survival and, regardless of politics, the best army to be loyal to was the army marching down the road toward them. Their only real hope was that the officer in charge was a man of honor. This was often not the case.

It was difficult for women to assert themselves in the 18th-century, even in a society that was brutalized and deprived by war. But many found a way. In 1780, General Washington reported to Congress that his army was basically starving, naked, and a very long time had passed since the soldiers were last paid. If relief didn't come soon he feared that he would lose his army altogether. Esther Reed, wife of Edmund Reed, the governor of Pennsylvania, had spent most of the war alone while her husband was away with Washington. During his absence, Mrs. Reed lost a child to smallpox, had been harassed by Loyalists and British soldiers, and was now recovering from smallpox herself. Esther imagined that if she was enduring such hardships then what must other men and women be going through under camp conditions. She would summon the wealthiest women in the city to help raise money for the troops. Her group printed broadcasts stating their intentions and then personally passed the notices door-to-door. By the end of their campaign, the Women's Association of Philadelphia reported to Washington that they had

A RARE CASE OF JUSTICE

Elizabeth "Mumbet" Freeman was a slave woman in Massachusetts who was struck with a hot fireplace shovel by her owner, Hannah Ashely, for shielding a younger slave girl from her blows. Freeman found a willing lawyer and sued Ashley for her freedom under the laws allowed by the Massachusetts constitution. The document, drafted by John Adams in 1779 and adopted by the state legislature in 1780, clearly states that "all men are born free and equal." Freeman had already suffered the loss of her enslaved husband, who was killed fighting against the British for the liberty of others. In August 1781, the court found in favor of Mumbet and granted her freedom, as well as a financial settlement. The Ashley's were made to pay for all legal fees.

Elizabeth "Mumbet" Freeman

raised $300,000 in Continental paper money – approximately $7,500 in hard currency, which was a large sum in that day. Upon hearing of this, the ladies of New Jersey and Maryland followed suite. At Washington's insistence, the money was spent on heavy linen to make shirts for his troops. The ladies purchased the fabric and had the material sowed into shirts. Sadly, Esther's bout with smallpox was more than she could take. She died on September 18, 1780, at the age of 34. To ensure that the project would stay on course, Sarah Franklin Bache, daughter of Benjamin Franklin, stepped in to take over Mrs. Reed's duties. Thanks to these women over 2,000 shirts were delivered to Washington's troops by year's end.

THE WIVES OF WASHINGTON'S GENERALS

We read so many tales of the Revolutionary-era generals leading their armies in the field, but what of their wives? Martha Washington, for example, was known to be with her husband during the harsh winter months, as were many of his generals' wives (some of whom may have made better generals than Washington's generals!)

CATHERINE VAN RENSSELAER SCHUYLER was no stranger to war. When General Burgoyne's army bore down on the Schuyler farm in Albany, NY, Catherine raced from the safety of a military camp to set her fields on fire, barely escaping capture as she was only minutes ahead of the British army. When warned ahead of time that her mission was too dangerous, Catherine laughed and said, "A general's wife *and* afraid - ridiculous!

LADY SARAH LIVINGSTON ALEXANDER STIRLING came from one of the wealthiest families in the colonies, but the war and bad debts would rob the Stirlings of their vast fortunes. After the war Congress denied her any pension because General Stirling had died of natural causes before the war had ended.

LUCY KNOX came from a very influential family of Loyalists. Her father was the Royal Secretary of the colony of Massachusetts. They abandoned Lucy and went back to England, never to speak to her again

DEBORAH PUTNAM not only ran the farm while her husband was away, but their tavern as well. Her health failed her on October 14, 1777, when the grief of losing her 17 year-old son overwhelmed her. She was with General Putnam at the time.

KITTY GREENE was easily the favorite of the soldiers and women alike when the wives of Washington's generals came to the winter camps. Full of fun and frivolous at heart, Washington often danced with Mrs. Greene when Martha took a breather.

POLLY WAYNE had a tough life and an even tougher husband. Even knowing that she had been very ill, General "Mad Anthony" Wayne writes to Polly in June 1777, saying that she must "get in your harvest yourself," or get help from the neighbors. He felt that prices that winter would be high and he didn't want to lose any of the profits paying off sharecroppers. He then let her know that she wasn't doing a good enough job with their daughters' education.

REBECCA CALHOUN PICKENS was well educated and possessed expert skills on horseback and with a rifle. Living in the Carolina backcountry was the most feared existence for a woman and small children. Many times she was forced to hide the family in the swampy woods for days or, if there was time, run to the local blockhouse for safety.

MARY GATES was born in England and the sincerity of her loyalty to the cause of independence has come under question. She appeared to be not near as interested in independence as she was her husband's success. Historians have often raised the same question about General Gates himself!

MARY WOOSTER supported her husband when he refused a commission as a British officer once the war broke out, and she continued to support him when he reached into their own funds to pay the men in his army. In 1779, she stayed behind to care for sick soldiers in her home, even while a British army was approaching the area.

Regardless of which colony these women and their families lived - whether rural or city - or even which side of the war they were on, the home front existence during the American Revolution was fragile, at best, for most; traumatic and horrifying for others. But once the battlefield itself battered down the front door, their lives were never the same.

When the Home Front Became a Battlefield

Every British colony in North America, from the Floridas to the Canadian colonies of Quebec and Nova Scotia, experienced military activity during the American Revolution. It might have been in a rural setting near small farms or in occupied cities like Boston, Savannah, or Charleston. Women who remained in their homes when war came to their door steps demonstrated their grit and determination many times over. Few regions experienced the viciousness of the southern backcountry, but these women were rough and rugged frontier folk long before a declared war came their way. Nancy Hart was just such a woman, living by the Broad River in the backcountry of Georgia. Known as "War Woman," or Wahatche, by the Cherokee people, Hart was a large woman and a skilled marksman and hunter. Her physical size and daunting courage gave her more than enough opportunity to dress as a man and act with a "simple-minded" manner, then wonder into Loyalist camps and British-held towns where she gathered information. She would then pass-on was she learned to Elijah Clark's Georgia militia. Her real notoriety, however, came from what was later known as a "Nancy Hart Dinner Party."

"Nancy Hart Dinner Party"

Six British soldiers had come demanding information about a local rebel outfit. When Nancy claimed to know nothing, they shot one of her turkeys, ordered her to cook it, and then bragged about killing one of her neighbors. Nancy calmly prepared their meal and kept plenty of liquor flowing. As the men were seated she had them place their firearms in a corner. At some point, Nancy grabbed the nearest rifle and killed the man closest to her. She then proceeded to take a second rifle and shot the next man. As she grabbed a third gun and drew down on another hapless soldier, they knew that she meant business and held their seats. It didn't take long for Nancy's daughter to gather her father and his rebel comrades. Typical of the style of warfare in the southern backcountry, the five men were hung as murderers for their treachery against the Hart's neighbor. Nancy became the only woman in Georgia history to have a county named in her honor. War Woman Creek, GA, was also named after Nancy to commemorate her bravery.

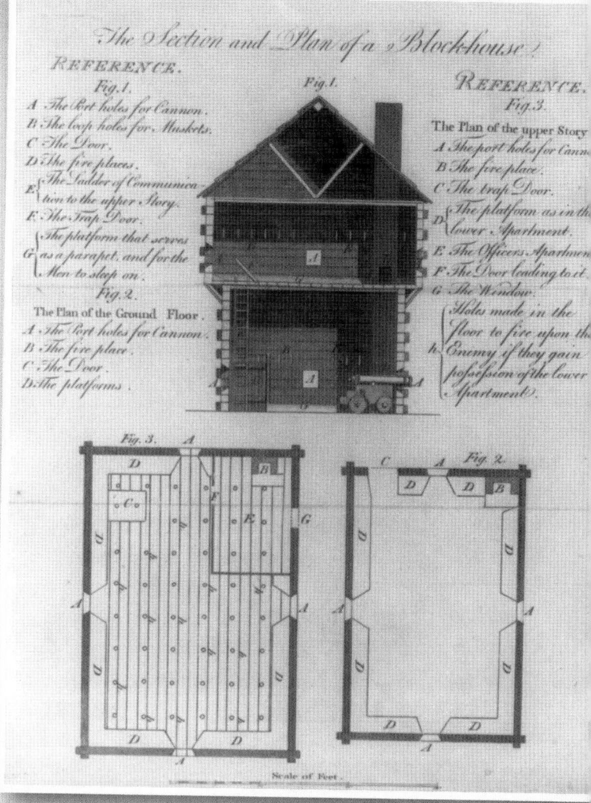

Cut-away diagram of a blockhouse

But the southern backcountry wasn't the only region where women put their lives on the line to help protect their homes and families from attack. Elizabeth Shell lived with her husband and sons in the frontier lands of New York. The Shells built a tiny fortress, or blockhouse, on their property to protect them when Loyalist militia and Indian allies attacked. Once inside the blockhouse, Elizabeth loaded muskets and rifles for her husband and sons to fire. On one occasion, attackers kept getting close enough to thrust their gun barrels through the loopholes of the blockhouse in order to shoot the family at point-blank range. Like something out of a cartoon, five times a gun barrel was shoved through a loophole and five times Elizabeth brought her ax down on the gun barrel hard enough to bend it, making it useless. None of her men were harmed on that day!

And it wasn't just the rugged frontier women who understood the sacrifices made when armies marched onto their lands and occupied their homes. Rebecca Motte was an extremely wealthy landowner from Charleston who was driven one-by-one from each of her vast estates as the British moved through South Carolina. After the fall of Camden, SC, in 1781, British general Lord Rawdon turned his troops to relieve the 165-man garrison stationed at an outpost that the British had established at Mrs. Motte's last remaining mansion. But a rebel army under the command of General Francis Marion, the "Swamp Fox," had other ideas. Marion set up camp across a gully from the Motte's plantation to attack the outpost before Lord Rawdon's reinforcements could arrive. Seeing what was happening, the British holding Mrs. Motte's estate sent all of the women out to the rebel camp for their own protection against the ensuing battle. Many of the British soldiers chuckled over the fact that

Making any sacrifice for independence

Rebecca's mother cradled an old Indian bow and a handful of filthy homemade arrows. If that was how the rebels planned to win the war, then let them come! Once the ladies were safe within the American camp, Lt. Colonel "Lighthorse Harry" Lee explained to Mrs. Motte that he had no choice but to burn her home in order to remove the British garrison. He knew it was her last residence on earth, one in which he had been a guest many times. Rebecca calmly went to her tent and returned with her mother's bow and arrows – they were filthy because she had smeared them with tar and gunpowder. Rebecca had already determined that if her home needed to be burned for the cause of liberty, then so be it.

Some of the events that took place seemed almost comical, but only after the fact. Grace and Rachel Martin were sisters-in-law whose husbands fought with Nathanial Greene's army. The women lived with their mother-in-law not far from the fort at Ninety-Six, South Carolina. The Martin homestead fronted the post road from Ninety-Six to Savannah and it wasn't unusual for the women to see soldiers and armies from both sides trudge by. On one occasion, word traveled the post road that a king's messenger was due that night, escorted by two British officers. The Martin girls put on their husbands' uniforms that had been left for laundering and repair, then laid in wait. The girls jumped out, put on their deepest husky voices, and demanded the letters carried by the courier. Caught completely by surprise, the three men eagerly gave up their dispatches and rode back the way they came. The girls made off for their cabin down a short-cut path and were there, looking pretty, when the three men stopped to ask for a meal and place to stay for the night.

Certainly, though, this type of home

front encounter affected more than just the families of those of English descent and who supported the rebellion. Molly Brandt was born into the Wolf Clan of the Mohawk Indian tribe in upper New York. Her step-father was a Mohawk sachem of the Turtle Clan who dressed and lived as a European. Molly was brought up with a European education and married an English nobleman, Sir William Johnson, who would become the Superintendent of the Northern Indian District. In 1774, Sir William died, leaving Molly with eight children to care for on the eve of the Revolution. Like the Cherokee, Mohawk women played important roles in tribal matters. Molly Brandt was already a politically powerful person in her own right, and a very successful trader and businesswoman. Throughout the war she continued to represent her people to the British government and worked tirelessly to keep the Mohawk aligned with Great Britain. As Loyalist refugees passed through the Mohawk Valley on their way to Canada, Molly would provide them a safe place to hide, find food, and replenish supplies. She stayed in the Mohawk Valley longer than most, but by 1777, the valley was no longer safe as rebel armies increasingly gained more ground in the region. Having moved to Canada, Molly continued to travel into the Mohawk-held areas of upstate New York to keep the alliance strong with Britain. By the end of the war all of the Iroquois nations and tribes who were

THEY DID WHAT THEY COULD

During the American Revolution some women risked their lives and some risked their fortunes; others risked their health. But in all cases they did what they could do. Elizabeth Steele, a tavern owner in South Carolina, gave her entire life's savings to Nathaniel Greene when he needed supplies in order to keep his army in the field, knowing that she would never see the money again. Catherine Moore Barry, another Carolinian, came to the aid of General Daniel Morgan at the Battle of the Cowpens by riding far and wide to recruit local men to join the rebel ranks. In New Hampshire, Molly Stark, the wife of General John Stark, oversaw many of the medical duties within the army camp and risked her health to personally administer care to 20 smallpox-stricken soldiers. Elizabeth Jackson, the mother of future president Andrew Jackson, died from the multiple diseases that she caught while caring for the sick and dying on a British prison ship. As the country song says, "All gave some and some gave all."

NINETY SIX

There are some unusual names for towns in the United States, but perhaps none more curious than the village of Ninety Six, South Carolina. There are several stories about how the town came to be called Ninety Six, but according to the town itself, the name most likely comes from when an Indian girl named Issaqueena (Cateechee) rode her horse 96 miles from Keowee, the capital of the Cherokee nation, to an outpost run by Robert Goudy to warn of an impending attack. By the time of the American Revolution, Ninety Six was an important hub in the Indian trade. In fact, it's believed that the first land battle in the southern colonies was fought at Ninety Six from November 19-21, 1775. Ninety Six became a hotbed of military activity, especially once Nathaniel Greene began his war-of-attrition against superior British forces, from 1780 to 1781. Today, Ninety Six is one of the American Revolution's hidden gems and should be on everyone's list of "must visit" Revolutionary War sites.

REVOLUTION OR CIVIL WAR?

Backcountry fighting in the southern colonies during the American Revolution was so vicious that many describe it as more of a civil war, rather than just the actions of a revolt. But what's the difference, you say? A revolt is when a group rises up against their authority, which in this case was the established government of Great Britain. Typically, if the revolt fails then it's forever known in history as just that, a revolt. If the revolt succeeds, as it did in the American colonies, France, and Haiti a few years later, then it's typically referred to as a revolution. But when within a single nation or empire at least two organized factions build armies in order to gain or maintain control of that country - or at least a portion of it - it's known as a civil war. Technically, the Russian Revolution became a civil war once the established government, the monarchy, was overthrown in 1917; civil war then raged until 1920. Regardless, the correct term for a person who is in rebellion against their government is "rebel." But let's be honest, "Patriot" just sounds better.

loyal to the Crown were forced to live in Canada. The Iroquois felt betrayed by Britain, however, because they had no representation at the 1783 Treaty of Paris. Frustrated, Molly and her family returned to their time-honored ways, speaking only their native tongue and wearing traditional Mohawk clothing.

Another woman in the Mohawk Valley who stood firm in her political beliefs and paid a dear price was Sarah Kast McGinnis. Sarah was not a Native American, but grew up with Mohawk children, learning their language and customs. Like Molly Brandt, she remained loyal to king and country and was relied upon heavily by the local British authorities to help keep other Mohawk loyal as well. Sarah's loyalty to the Crown cost her all of her earthly possessions – her land, trading post, and home – as well as a daughter who died in a rebel prison where they were both held captive. Eventually, Sarah was liberated by Mohawk warriors as they retreated into Canada with British troops. After the war her restitution by the British government was meager and no reimbursement was given for the land that she lost.

For some women it didn't matter what they did, they were doomed to be on the wrong side of everything. Theodosia Prevost's ties to the Crown ran very deep. She was the wife of a British officer, Major James Mark Prevost, who saw action throughout the South and was the royal governor of Georgia in 1778. His brother was a British general and the governor of Jamaica. The Major and Mrs. Prevost invested in vast estates in New York before settling down in New Jersey. But when New Jersey fell to the rebellion, Theodosia found that the best way to preserve her family's holdings was to cheerfully open her homes and lands to the armies and officers in charge, including George Washington, James Monroe, the Marquis de Lafayette, and Alexander Hamilton. Even with that, the New Jersey Court of Common Pleas insisted that her lands be confiscated and, in 1780, she lost her appeal. Widowed in 1781, Theodosia would soon marry one of the officers she had met when his regiment stopped at her property while traveling to Valley Forge. His name was Aaron Burr, who would later become Thomas Jefferson's vice president and, in 1804, kill Alexander Hamilton in a duel. Once again, as the result of her husband's actions and politics, Theodosia would find herself a social outcast – even though she herself had never offended anyone.

The case of Theodosia Prevost wasn't unusual. When it came to political leanings, Revolutionary-era women were typically associated with whatever side of the conflict that their husbands and/or fathers prescribed. In the instance of Hannah Caldwell, whose husband preached independence from his pulpit at the First Presbyterian Church in Bordentown, NJ, her guilt-by-association became deadly. When Hessian general Baron Wilhelm Von Knyphausen landed British troops at Elizabethtown on June 6, 1780, rebels like Parson Caldwell sent their families away for protection while they themselves disappeared into the woods. Hannah, however, remained in her home with her eight month old baby, two other very small children, and a nurse. She believed that an innocent woman with a baby in her arms was safe from harm. She was wrong. The rage felt by British troops against her husband was so strong that soldiers approached the

THE BELOVED WOMAN

In July 1781, a Cherokee woman named Nanye'hi, was selected to lead negotiations between the Cherokee people and victorious colonial leaders in the southern backcountry. Known for decades as "the Beloved Woman" by her people, Nanye'hi delivered these words to those in attendance: "You know that women are always looked upon as nothing; but we are your mothers; you are our sons. Our cry is all for peace; let it continue. This peace must last forever. Let your women's sons be ours. Let our sons be yours. Let your women hear our words." Unfortunately, Nanye'hi was being poetic in her description of women's role in Cherokee culture when she described women a being looked upon as nothing. What she didn't understand was that in Anglo culture this description was completely accurate. Her real plea at these negotiations was that these men would take her words and peace offerings back to the real decision makers - the mothers - and let them know that the Cherokee were a peaceful people. This message, of course, would never be delivered as intended.

There is now a musical about Nanye-hi!

home, shot and killed Hannah – who was still holding the baby – then stripped her corpse and robbed it of any valuables as officers looked on.

News of British atrocities traveled quickly throughout the colonies. Independence-minded colonists suspected anyone who was not a proclaimed fire-breathing rebel. Retribution toward Loyalists was quick and quite often ended in brutal beatings and/or a "suit of tar and feathers." Many suffered for

Discipline under fire

no reason other than vicious rumors. From December 6, 1776 to June 14, 1777, Margaret Morris recorded the staggering events that took place in Burlington, NJ. This Quaker widow was caught in a net of neutrality that would put her and her children constantly in harm's way, as she was allied to neither side and distrusted by both. Tension mounted as reports, letters, and post riders would insist that Hessian troops were only hours away...every day. Then, on December 11, after five agonizing days of watching friends and neighbors fleeing the town in a frenzy, 600 rebel troops in retreat filled the streets, with the Hessians close behind. Once the Hessians arrived, they searched homes for rebel belongings, but little more. They realized that a fleet of small rebel ships (referred to in the journal as gondolas and gallies) anchored in the Delaware River. Not wishing the people of town harmed, the Hessian commander sent his troops away from occupied homes. However, "the people of the gallies" believed the houses to be occupied by Hessians

"MAMMY KATE"

Mammy Kate and her husband, Daddy Jack, were two slaves owned by Governor Stephen Heard of Georgia. When Georgia was taken by British forces in 1778, Gov. Heard went from politician to freedom fighter. But when Heard was captured at the Battle of Kettle Creek on February 14, 1779, he was moved to Augusta and condemned to death. Kate and Jack devised a plan to aid their owner before his execution could take place. Since Heard was a small man and Mammy Kate a very large woman, Kate was said to have entered the prison with a large basket filled with fresh laundry for the condemned prisoner. Once in his cell, Kate removed most of the pile of clothes, put Heard in the basket, covered him up, and carried him out like she hadn't a care in the world. Once she reached the woods with her heavy basket, Daddy Jack was waiting with horses to whisk the governor to safety. This is truly an account where fact can be more incredible than fiction!

and soon bombarded Burlington and threatened to set fire to the town. Shortly after, "Tory-hunters" pounded on doors, demanding to search homes for anyone loyal to the king. Margaret stood helpless by her sick, frightened children as her home was searched, but they had good reason to be so scared. Margaret was hiding Dr. Jonathan Odell, a Loyalist, in a secret room, for no other reason than the sake of human compassion. Because of her religious-based neutrality, Margaret's journal – written under the worst of circumstances – provides crisp reports of daily events with none of the exaggeration for superiority of cause found in so many similar accounts.

In March 1777, word was sent house-to-house throughout the townships of Pepperell, Groton, and Hollis, MA, that a small body of British regulars led by one of the locally-born officers, Captain Leonard Whiting, would come through the area looking for rebel sympathizers. It was also said that Captain Whiting carried dispatches of some importance. With their men away at war, some 30 – 40 women of the region joined Sarah Shattuck and Prudence Wright in doing something about it. The ladies dressed as men and positioned themselves to defend Jewett's Bridge, the only means for crossing the Nashua River into their region. As it turned out there were only two British officers, rather than a body of soldiers, and one of them was Mrs. Wright's brother. Some say that he recognized his sister's voice and rather than engage her in battle he turned his horse and fled. Captain Whiting drew his pistol to fire but was promptly dragged from his horse and wrestled to the ground. The ladies found in his boots the dispatches he carried, then trussed him up tightly and marched him back to Pepperell to be jailed. One can only wonder at what point the good captain realized that it was the women of his home town who had captured him!

Dicey Langston, a fiery woman from the backcountry of South Carolina, was

Husky-voiced and brave!

RACHAEL SILVERTHORN

Rachel Silverthorn lived in the rural regions of Pennsylvania - far enough west that troop protection against Native American attacks was rarely afforded by the British or colonial militia. This was frontier living and fighting at its harshest. In the summer of 1778, tensions were at a peak and settlers often sought refuge at local forts. Sometimes riders arrived in time to warn folks on their farms, sometimes they didn't. It was during this time that a large party of warriors were bearing down on Fort Muncy. There was too little time to warn those in the outlying farms and there were no men in the fort willing to ride out on a suicide mission, even after the commanding officer offered his own horse. Before anyone knew what was happening, Rachel Silverthorn mounted the horse and rode off. Her ride saved many lives and has been known since as the "Big Runaway."

hiding one of her brother's rifles. Before long a group of wary looking men came into her home demanding the rifle. Dicey knew that there was a secret sign, but they refused to show her the signal. She produced the gun but wouldn't hand it over until she was given the secret sign. Laughing, the leader told her what a fool she was for now they had her and the gun in their possession. Dicey whipped the rifle around, cocking it as she put the muzzle in his face, and said, *"If the gun is in your possession, take charge of her!"*

Tormentors on both sides knew no bounds when it came to emotional cruelty for those who stayed behind while husbands were away at war. Dorcas Richardson's husband, rebel Major Richard Richardson, had been taken prisoner after the British captured Charleston in 1780. Richardson was sent to a disease-ridden prison where he caught smallpox, but eventually gained enough strength to escape. The major made his way home but was forced to live in the swamps nearby, as British dragoons were quartered at his own plantation. Once news of Richardson's escape and the "Dead or Alive" bounty was posted, British officers and Loyalists harassed Dorcas for her husband's whereabouts. She was insulted, threatened, and her littlest children questioned. Men would boast in the presence of the family what they would do to Major Richardson once he was caught, while others would claim that they had found and hung him, or show up with swords dripping with blood that was said to be his – all in the hopes that Dorcas would run to his hideout so they could follow. Days would go by before she could take him food and learn for herself that he was safe. One young man whom Dorcas knew well was captured and hung from a tree near her front door. Soldiers taunted her with shouts that her husband would be next. But she remained strong while her husband gathered rebel fighters around him in the swamp. Major Richardson and his men eventually joined forces with the "Swamp Fox" and re-entered the war thanks to his wife's grit under such terrible circumstances. Dorcas Richardson was 93 when she died.

General Francis Marion, the "Swamp Fox," has his prey!

HOW MANY BRITISH COLONIES WERE THERE?

When fighting broke out in 1775, there were 33 colonies in the British Americas, spanning from Nova Scotia in the north down to Grenada in the south Caribbean. We forget that in North America alone there were 17 British colonies, including the 13 in rebellion, East Florida, West Florida, Quebec, and Nova Scotia. There were 16 colonies in the British West Indies, as well, where 60% of the British military was stationed during the war to protect the production of sugar.

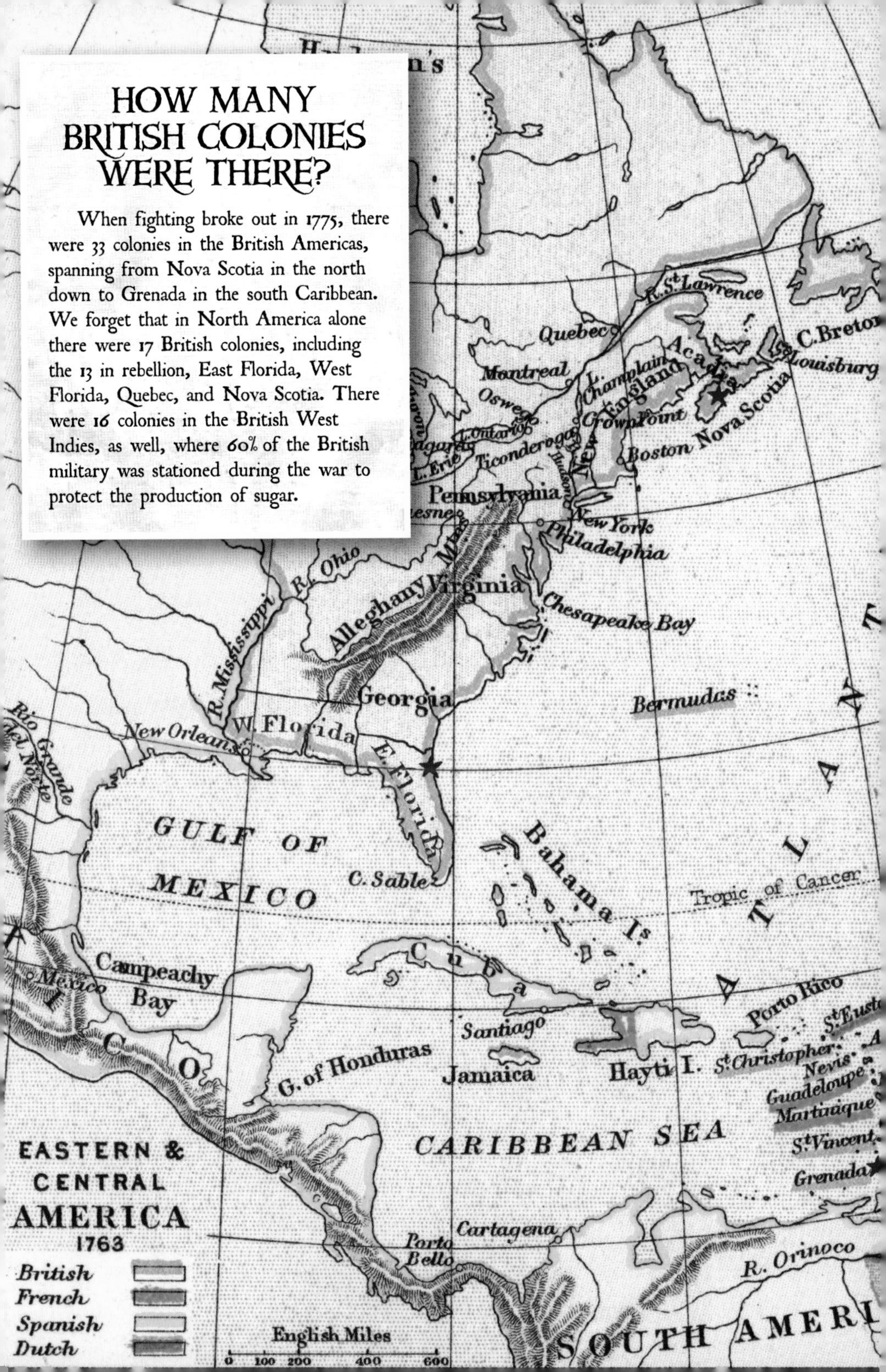

MIDNIGHT RIDES!

Few people understand that Paul Revere was not the only person who made a daring "midnight ride" to warn of British attack. In fact, Revere wasn't even alone on the night that made him famous. In addition to William Dawes and Dr. Samuel Prescott, many other riders scattered throughout the countryside, including Israel Bissell, who rode from Watertown, MA, to Philadelphia - 345 miles, taking over four days. Paul Revere, while considered the primary figure on this historic night, was captured after riding only 13 miles. In 1781, Virginia's Captain Jack Jouett covered approximately 40 miles in the dead of night through rugged terrain to avoid main roads choked with British patrols to warn a Congress-in-hiding of a British approach. In Connecticut a similar story is told about a 40-mile long midnight ride that took place in April 1777. A rider was dispatched from the town of Danbury during a torrential rainstorm that muddied the roads to the point of being extremely dangerous on such a dark, moonless night. The British were near Danbury and intended to set fire to the town. The rider crossed the border into New York, alarming 400 militiamen from both colonies along the way that Danbury was in need. Too late to save Danbury, the army drew courage from having gathered so many men at a minute's notice and dug-in at Ridgefield, CT. There they turned the advancing British army that otherwise would have continued into New York. General Washington publically commended the rider for their service to the cause of independence. The name of the hero who made this daring ride was Sybil Ludington, a 16 year old girl whose father was a colonel in the Connecticut militia. Like many young girls who could ride, Sybil continued to serve the army throughout the war as a messenger. So why haven't the names of Dawes, Prescott, Jouett, Bissell, and Ludington received the same historical fame as Revere? Perhaps it's because they didn't gain the good fortune of having a famous poem written about them by Henry Wadsworth Longfellow. After all, "Listen my children and you shall hear" is such a great opening line...but it doesn't rhyme with Ludington!

OTHER GREAT RIDES

BETSY DOWDY'S "midnight ride" on December 8-9, 1775, carried her 50 miles, swimming the Currituck Sound along the way, to raise troops for the rebel victory at Great Bridge, VA. DEBORAH CHAMPION was the daughter of Henry Champion, a veteran of the French and Indian War who was now the Commissary General of the American Army. Her father needed dispatches from New London, CT, delivered to General Washington in Boston. Though the ride was over 100 miles, he sent his own daughter, showing to what lengths a general in the Continental Army would go to gain independence. MARY McCLURE was on her farm with her two younger sons who were home from General Sumter's camp to melt down pewter for bullets. The boys were discovered by British scouts and taken to be executed the next day. While in her home, Mary overheard British plans for the continuing campaign. Mary understood the severity of her boys' situation, but also knew that Sumter needed this information. She rode that night to Sumter's camp to warn him of British intentions. The next morning the redcoats were caught sound asleep by Sumter's army and the boys lives saved. EMILY GEIGER stepped forward in May 1781, when General Nathaniel Greene was faced with making a scattered retreat from South Carolina up to North Carolina and on to Virginia. To keep this from happening, Greene needed reinforcements from General Thomas Sumter who was fifty miles away and it was Emily who volunteered to carry the message. The young girl headed from Greene's camp in the wrong direction to avoid suspicion, then made a wide loop back toward Sumter's army. Around noon the next day she ran into British patrols and became so flustered that she could barely speak. The soldiers took her captive and locked her away, where Emily then ate the message intended for Sumter. A Loyalist woman came into the room to search the girl, but found nothing and scolded the soldiers for scaring her so badly. Emily was released, made off in the wrong direction, again, and then circled around toward Sumter's camp. Sumter and Greene would combine their armies and defeat the British at Eutaw Springs, S.C.

In Harm's Way

Not all families in the Revolutionary era lived on frontier farms and fertile plantations, or had the luxury of owning businesses, shops, or taverns. Not all women had the means to support themselves and their children while the men in their lives were away at war...or because of the war, had gone away forever. There were many families that simply couldn't survive without the effort of every member of the entire family to help out. For this reason, many women and children went to war with the men and older boys, doing whatever was required to earn their keep. The women understood the skills of cooking and caring for the family and home, but few were prepared to perform these tasks for thousands of people in an open-air setting. Even fewer had lived in a military encampment where "caring" for someone often meant dealing with outbreaks of deadly diseases, bandaging horrific wounds, assisting with an amputation, or helping some mother's son die as comfortably as possible. But regardless of their state of preparedness, the one common bond among them all was that they were simply trying to stay alive, and keep their children alive, until the madness was over.

These women and their families were known as "camp followers." In the 19th and early 20th centuries this term carried a very negative connotation, but in the 18th century and earlier that wasn't the case. While in camp, the women and

BARONESS UNDER FIRE

Baroness Friederike von Riedesel could have remained in the luxury of her estates in Brunswick, Germany, when Maj. General Friedrich Adolph Riedesel's troops shipped-out for North America. Instead, she chose to gather her small children and follow her husband. General Riedesel was placed in command of all Hessian troops and Indian allies in the Northern Campaign that ended in defeat at the Battle of Saratoga. As the battle worsened the Baroness was encouraged to take her family and other camp followers to a house now known as the Marshall House. Before long, wounded soldiers began filling the house. The result was a nightmare: "Immediately after our arrival a frightful cannonade began, principally directed against the house in which we had sought shelter, probably because the enemy believed, from seeing so many people flocking around it, that all the generals made it their head-quarters." The siege lasted six days, leaving those in the cellar of the Marshall House no food, water, toiletries, or proper medical care for the wounded and dying. Only a British surrender brought an end to their nightmare.

Frederika Charlotte Louise von Massow, Baroness Riedesel

their children often lived as a family alongside their soldiers. Everyone knew their duties and everyone had a duty to do. When on the move, the families followed at the army's rear, sometimes as much as an hour behind. One reason for this was to keep them out of harm's way in case of ambush or attack. It also gave them plenty of notice if a retreat was coming their way. Another reason was that they were often slower in their pace. Almost comically, while Washington complained often of their slowness, he wouldn't allow women and children to ride in any of the wagons – and yet his most consistent complaint about camp followers was how they were constantly found occupying a place in the wagons! He may have been the Commander-in-Chief of the entire Continental Army, but the women understood that it was they who would prepare his meals and tend to his wounded.

Camp followers were so prevalent that early on Washington addressed the idea of putting them to use in the war effort. He understood their value, for example, in meeting the demands for medical care for his soldiers, freeing up men from such duties as medics and nurses so that they could better serve on the battle lines. Occasionally referring to these ladies as the "Women of the Army," a significant part of Washington's solution was to assign them official duties, such as nurses, cooks, laundresses, water bearers, even baby sitters and nannies for other women who were going about their own duties. Children pitched-in to help where they could, as many already knew how to make rifle and musket cartridges.

It may be argued that the medical corps was the most important assignment for women in the camps. Congress authorized the army to employ one nurse for each 10 sick or wounded soldiers.

"Aim for the house!"

Camp followers resting at Black-Heath, 1780

Since much of the medical care of the day was provided in the home by women, professional training for nurses was virtually nonexistent. Whatever nursing skills they brought to the war effort came from much smaller concerns on the home front or were learned on the run as needs arose. Respected estimates for the number of nurses during the Revolution have been put as high as 20,000. And they were paid for their services, at first earning two dollars per month and one daily ration of food. By 1777, their wages had increased to eight dollars per month but still only one ration of food each day. While we might hope that this increase in earnings was the result of a realization for the importance of their duties, it's just as likely that it only represents the rapid inflation of the Continental dollar.

Not all of the "Women of the Army" came into camp to cook or dress wounds – they certainly had no intention of being a laundress or nanny. They came to fight. As simple as this sounds, it was anything but a simple matter. It just wasn't socially acceptable. But fight they would.

The topic of women serving in the military, and in what capacity, has been a heated debate throughout American history. It has only been since 2015 that combat trained women in the United States military have been allowed to put this training to use by actually serving as front line combatants. One might think that during the American Revolution the Continental Army, and especially local and state militias, would take anyone who could hold their own in the heat of battle. Such was not the case. But that doesn't mean that women who supported the cause of independence – and wanted to be in the thick of the fight – would not find a way to make that happen. While there's no doubt there are many stories of women disguising themselves as men in order to fight, some disguised themselves so well that it was never known that they had a story to tell. For others, we only learned of their well-intended deceptions after their deaths. Sally St. Clair, who's described as a "creole" girl, enlisted as a man in a South Carolina regiment in order to be with her beau. Her reasoning for the deception could have been that as a man of color she would have been better treated in the army than a darker-skinned camp follower. Whatever her thinking, Sally was killed in the Battle of Savannah in 1778, and only then was it discovered that she was a woman. Elizabeth Gilmore of Northumberland County Pennsylvania enlisted as a private in the Continental Army and drew pay. She was also listed among the "Rangers on the Frontier," but little else is known.

Anna Maria Lane joined her husband when he enlisted in the Continental Army in 1776, but not as a cook or camp nurse. Anna put on men's clothing and enlisted to fight at his side. The Lanes were with Washington in New Jersey and Pennsylvania before Anna's military career was cut short at the Battle of Germantown, PA, in 1777. A wound to her leg was so severe that she would remain lame for the rest of her life. John Lane stayed with the army and was at the Siege of Savannah in 1778, where he too was wounded. By good fortune, the Lanes found one another after John had healed enough to return to their homeland of Virginia.

PRISON SHIPS

With the early military campaigns of Long Island came the quick understanding that the British had no real plan for accommodating prisoners of war. A deadly solution was soon found: the prison ship. Simply put, these were little more than death and disease afloat. Horribly overcrowded and vermin-ridden, the prisoners cooked rancid food, prepared in noxious pots, boiled in the same stagnant seawater in which their refuse was dumped. Small pox and deadly "camp fevers" were rampant. Women, like Elizabeth Burgin, followed in the footsteps of Elizabeth Jackson and risked their lives caring for these poor men. Mrs. Burgin, however, became part of a plot by rebel leaders on Long Island. As the story goes, Elizabeth would row her boat out to one of the near-by prison ships, slip a sleeping potion into the guards' beer, then tend to the prisoners. Once the guards were asleep she would get as many of the wretched men into her boat as she dared and row ashore. Over time, Elizabeth helped approximately 200 men escape. To lend credence to her story, we know that the British put a £200 bounty on her head (the equivalent of about 20 years pay for the common soldier!). Elizabeth was also awarded a pension at the end of the war by George Washington.

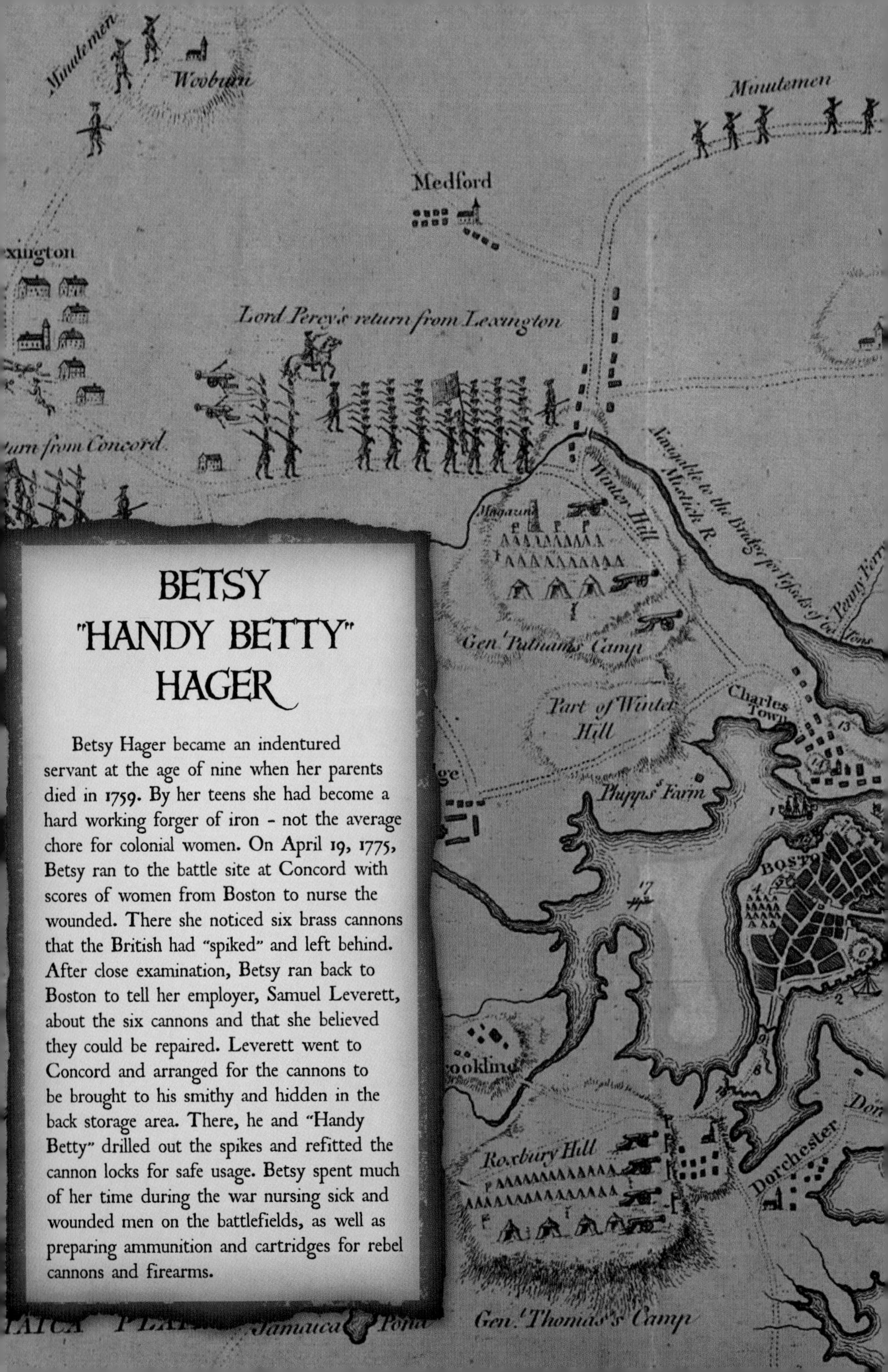

BETSY "HANDY BETTY" HAGER

Betsy Hager became an indentured servant at the age of nine when her parents died in 1759. By her teens she had become a hard working forger of iron - not the average chore for colonial women. On April 19, 1775, Betsy ran to the battle site at Concord with scores of women from Boston to nurse the wounded. There she noticed six brass cannons that the British had "spiked" and left behind. After close examination, Betsy ran back to Boston to tell her employer, Samuel Leverett, about the six cannons and that she believed they could be repaired. Leverett went to Concord and arranged for the cannons to be brought to his smithy and hidden in the back storage area. There, he and "Handy Betty" drilled out the spikes and refitted the cannon locks for safe usage. Betsy spent much of her time during the war nursing sick and wounded men on the battlefields, as well as preparing ammunition and cartridges for rebel cannons and firearms.

MOLLY *PITCHERS* - more than *one*?

Margaret Corbin (Fort Washington, L.I., 1776) and Mary Hays McCauley (Monmouth Courthouse, 1778) have both been remembered by history as the famous Molly Pitcher.

After watching her husband cut down by a musket ball, Margaret Corbin took over his cannon duties, but she too was injured badly enough that a report by Congress in 1779 referred to her as "wounded and utterly disabled."

Mary Hays McCauley performed the same task when her husband was wounded too badly to continue at his cannon. Mary fought for hours, yet continued to carry water to other artillerymen while her own gun was being reloaded.

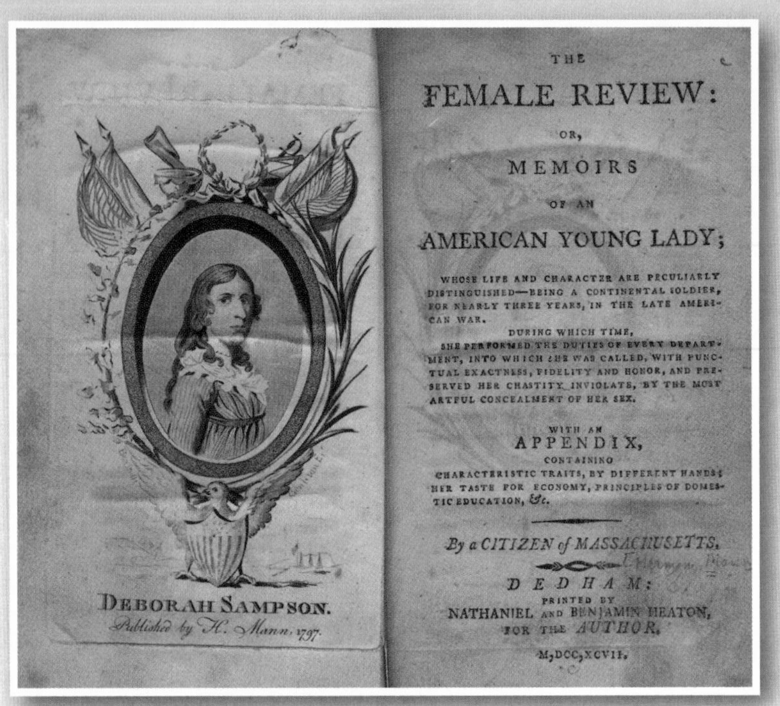

DEBORAH SAMPSON.
Published by H. Mann, 1797.

THE
FEMALE REVIEW:
OR,
MEMOIRS
OF AN
AMERICAN YOUNG LADY;

WHOSE LIFE AND CHARACTER ARE PECULIARLY DISTINGUISHED—BEING A CONTINENTAL SOLDIER, FOR NEARLY THREE YEARS, IN THE LATE AMERICAN WAR.
DURING WHICH TIME,
SHE PERFORMED THE DUTIES OF EVERY DEPARTMENT, INTO WHICH SHE WAS CALLED, WITH PUNCTUAL EXACTNESS, FIDELITY AND HONOR, AND PRESERVED HER CHASTITY INVIOLATE, BY THE MOST ARTFUL CONCEALMENT OF HER SEX.

WITH AN
APPENDIX,
CONTAINING
CHARACTERISTIC TRAITS, BY DIFFERENT HANDS; HER TASTE FOR ECONOMY, PRINCIPLES OF DOMESTIC EDUCATION, &c.

By a CITIZEN of MASSACHUSETTS.

DEDHAM:
PRINTED BY
NATHANIEL AND BENJAMIN HEATON,
FOR THE AUTHOR.
M,DCC,XCVII.

Rare copy of book about Deborah Sampson

On May 20, 1782, Robert Shurtleff enlisted in the private ranks of the Fourth Massachusetts Regiment of Foot under the command of Captain George Webb. He served with valor and without pay until the end of the war, but was eventually granted full compensation for his time in the army – even though it was known by that time that Robert Shurtleff was actually a woman named Deborah Samson. We tend to forget that fighting didn't end after the Battle of Yorktown in 1781, it just scaled down. Deborah saw action in the contested regions of New York, where Loyalist militias fought to the bitter end. Deborah was a credit to her regiment and was wounded on more than one occasion – including a saber slash to the head in hand-to-hand combat. Fortunately, when field physicians bandaged her head they failed to notice that she also had a musket ball wound to her thigh. Knowing that her secret would be discovered once the leg wound was examined, Deborah left the hospital, dug the bullet from her thigh with a small knife, and then stitched the wound herself. Her identity was only discovered later after she lost consciousness during a bout with fever and the attending doctor learned the truth. Nothing was said after her recovery, but she was sent immediately on a mission to deliver a message to General John Patterson. It was only after she delivered the note that Deborah realized that the message she carried was to inform the general that Robert Shurtleff was a woman – though a solider of great valor – a woman, nonetheless. Patterson allowed Deborah one last mission: to carry the same message to General Washington. Frightened and certainly tempted to desert, Deborah carried out her last order with honor. After reading the letter, Washington wrote out a letter of honorary discharge and gave Deborah

Extreme courage under fire!

enough money to make her way home. Later, President Washington invited Deborah to visit with him at the nation's capital. With the help of Paul Revere, Deborah would receive a pension for her services. She also became one the first women in American history to earn a living as a lecturer, traveling throughout New England and New York to tell of her many adventures. And how did she dress for these occasions? As, a man of course – in full military uniform.

But what drove these women to such intensive needs for secrecy? Was it fear of being bullied or molested in the ranks by the men? Was is concern that they might embarrass their families? There's no doubt that every woman who took such great strides to conceal their identities had their own reasons and concerns. But when we consider what happened to those women whose identities were discovered, the answer might be more obvious. Samuel Gay, for example, enlisted in the 1st Massachusetts Regiment, rose to the rank of corporal in just three weeks and then suddenly deserted. When he was caught soon after, it was discovered that Samuel Gay was actually Ann Bailey. Poor Ann was tried and sentenced to prison for two years – but not for desertion. Ann Baily, who only wanted to serve her country on the battlefield, was imprisoned on the charge of wearing men's clothing in public. Another woman, whose name isn't known, enlisted in the 1st New Jersey Regiment. When she was discovered, she was thrown out of the army and publically humiliated as her tormentors marched her through the nearest town, calling upon the town's people to heap insults and foul objects in her direction.

Every human being is different. Not every woman of the Revolutionary era was born to dress in lace and sew or cook for their husbands. Many of these women, just like those in our military today, simply wanted to serve their country in the manner they felt most capable – they wanted to fight. For that, we owe them our long-overdue respect and our admiration.

MRS DANIEL BOONE?

We've all heard the name of Daniel Boone, but what of the woman who married him - and at what cost? In 1773, Rebecca Boone would lose her oldest son in a battle with Indians on their first trip west. In 1774-1775, she and her children were left alone in the wilderness while Daniel was on an 800-mile surveying expedition. In 1776 she endured the horror of her daughter being kidnapped by Cherokee and Shawnee warriors. In 1778, Daniel was captured by the Shawnee and presumed dead. Rebecca returned to North Carolina. Almost one year later, Daniel showed up to take her back to Kentucky. One can only wonder if she would have gone had she known that she would soon lose another son in yet another fight with Native American warriors.

Spies!

George Washington has recently been referred to as a spy master – a title that was well deserved. During the French and Indian War, Washington's keen powers of observation were utilized on more than one occasion by his commanding officers. They would send him to a French fort or encampment, under a flag of truce, with a message that required a response. While waiting, Washington would casually make a mental note of everything he saw – everything! His years as a surveyor had prepared him for these missions and his recollections were of the finest details. But since Washington was in uniform and had been allowed to enter the enemy camp, what he did was considered to be an honorable form of spying. If he had been caught he would have received his enemy's scorn, but little more.

The Importance of Spies

Imagine fighting a battle with your eyes closed. Or planning a military campaign having no idea if your intended target is even in the area. This was what generals of the American Revolution were up against every day of the war - where is my enemy and what size and strength is their army? In an era of history when the most advanced technology for gathering strategic military information was to overhear conversations or physically intercept mail packets, spies would perform tremendous acts of courage and put themselves in harm's way, with little hope of rescue if caught. Then, of course, a spy had to engineer a safe and secretive way to get that information back to the generals in the field in order to spark victory and/or avoid disaster. Communication today, whether by cell phone, text, twitter, Facebook, emails, or snapchat, is available to billions of people, and information passed globally within seconds. Imagine what George Washington would have given for a simple set of walkie-talkies!

Hamilton and the Sentinel at Morristown

In more recent wars, such as WWII, spying became as much a cultural science as it was a test of nerves. For example, Europeans and Americans have different ways of handling their knives and forks during a meal, meaning that spies had to constantly be aware of their surroundings and not fall back into old habits and practices. If a spy claimed to be from Munich, Germany, they had to come prepared with the proper dialect and fashion nuances of Bavaria. But during the American Revolution, creating this type of diversion or disguise was much easier to do. On both sides of the war there were people who spoke with accents, whether it was British, colonial, Scottish, Irish, French, German, Dutch, or Scandinavian. The ideals of the American Revolution didn't divide people by nationalities, but rather by politics, so all sides in the war were made up of all peoples. The best disguise that a spy could possess – a disguise that Nathan Hale didn't have – was the ability to simply look like they belonged where ever they were; to blend into the woodwork, so to speak.

HONORABLE AND DISHONORABLE SPIES?

Most Americans are familiar with the name Nathan Hale, considered by many to be the American Revolution's most famous spy. He was also what would have been termed "dishonorable" in his mission. Not that he was a dishonorable person, but his mission was dishonorable due to its secrecy and the concealment of his identity. He was dressed as a civilian, pretending to be a Loyalist, and tried to disguise his purpose for being where he was. Unfortunately, he had not been properly trained in the better techniques of keeping his mission secretive. Rather than making casual mental notes of what he saw and committing the information to paper in the privacy of his lodgings, Hale was quite obvious in scribbling information down right on the spot when an army passed by or when he was near an encampment. Hale was so obvious in his methods that his career as a spy was possibly the shortest in history: he crossed the Long Island Sound from Connecticut on September 16, 1776; was spotted on September 19; under surveillance all day September 20; captured September 21; hung on September 22 - with all of the information he collected lost to the British.

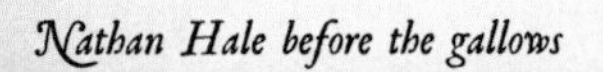
Nathan Hale before the gallows

For this reason, some of the best spies were women. For one thing, in Western civilization the Revolutionary era falls into what is known as the Age of Enlightenment. And yet, it was not believed that women had the mental or emotional stamina to tell lies and keep secrets...seriously. It was believed that women were too delicate and fragile, not to mention uneducated and foolish, to take on such dangerous tasks without completely falling apart during the mission. So right away, it becomes apparent that the best disguise for a spy was to be a woman. Take, for example, a simple house servant going about her chores without making a sound or bringing attention to herself in any way. Just quietly listening to everything being said around her.

Or perhaps the spy was a woman whose home was being occupied by British officers. Lydia Darragh and her husband William were a Quaker couple who lived in British-occupied Philadelphia in 1777. On the evening of December 2, an officer – none other than the British spy master, Major John André – was lodging at their home. André knocked on the Darragh's bedroom door and asked her to set up a room in the back of the house for a special meeting that night. Suspicious, Lydia sneaked down to listen at the door as orders from General Sir William Howe were read. She learned that British troops were leaving Philadelphia the next evening to surprise Washington's army at Whitemarsh, PA. Mrs. Darragh waited until the next morning, so as not to create suspicion, and requested official papers allowing her to walk to a flour mill outside of town for supplies. Once there, she dropped off her flour bags to be filled, continued on toward Whitemarsh until she was stopped by a rebel sentry, and conveyed her information. Lydia then walked back to the mill, picked up her loaded bags of flour, and headed home. When the British arrived at Whitemarsh, Washington was ready. Surprised, Howe sat for three days before finally returning to Philadelphia without a fight.

THE AGE OF ENLIGHTENMENT

Also known as the Age of Reason, this era of European history runs from approximately 1685 - 1815. It was during this time that great advances in science, philosophy, politics, mathematics, and communication were radically removed from the previous era, which basically stated that everything was the way that it is because that was God's will. As men made great gains in intellectual feats, reason slowly began to replace faith, especially in academic circles. Except, of course, when it came to things that couldn't be explained or reasoned-away... such as women. Men are still working on that one!

JUST A FEW WORDS ABOUT HER IS ALL WE HAVE...

"An order was drawn upon the Treasurer in favor of Miss Eleanor Hitchcock, for the sum of £12, in full of her account for her services in the years 1775 and 1776, in erecting at Cape Henlopen a large pole, and hoisting thereon from time to time two flags, as signals to vessels belonging to the bay and river Delaware, of the approach of the enemy, pursuant to instructions from the Committee of Safety..."
(Colonial Records of Pennsylvania)

But if being a simple working woman was a good disguise, being an old working woman was even better. Molly "Mom" Rinker was perfect. She was zealous in her stance for liberty, her family owned an inn in Philadelphia where British soldiers quartered and ate their meals, and she was smart as a whip. In fact, the age of "Mom" Rinker isn't known, but in every account of her activities she is described in the same manner: a little old, gray-haired lady. During the British occupation of Philadelphia, from 1777 through 1778, officers frequently gave and carried out orders or made plans around the dining table at the Rinker's inn. Typically, the Rinker's were ushered out of the room, with the exception of Mom, who stayed throughout the course of the meal in order to serve them food and drink – the "drink" part flowed freely. Each time such a meeting was held at their inn, Mom Rinker would spend the next day perched on the edge of a near-by bluff to knit. But inside wound balls of yarn were messages with the information she had overheard the night before. At some point Mom would "accidently" drop one of her knitting balls, watching helplessly as it would bound down the rock face and into the woods below... where Washington's couriers were waiting. No invisible ink. No clandestine meetings. A plan so simple that it was brilliant. Mom Rinker continued her work during the entire British occupation of Philadelphia. Her information is credited with altering the fate of the General John Armstrong's troops at the Battle of Germantown on October 4, 1777. While the encounter was a British victory, Armstrong stated later that his men would have been wiped-out without her report. "Mom Rinker's Rock" has since been honored with a statue and can be visited in Philadelphia today.

INVISIBLE INK... SERIOUSLY?

As "Hollywood" as it might sound, there truly was such a thing as invisible ink available during the American Revolution. On November 19, 1778, founding father John Jay wrote to Washington stating that a three-year experiment was positively concluded and "a mode of correspondence, which may be of use, provided proper agents could be obtained." As historian Alexander Rose reveals in his work, *Washington's Spies: The Story of America's First Spy Ring*, the "sympathetic ink" was created by mixing and dissolving "60 grains of gallic acid with 10 grains of powdered acacia." As for bringing the invisible ink back into view, "acquire 30 grains of ferrous sulphate and dissolve them in 8 ounces of distilled water." Can't get much simpler than that!

Without dependable information, New Yorkers woke up to this scene in July of 1776, without warning!

But utilizing working women as spies in this manner was only successful if the British just so happened to occupy a home where such a woman lived or worked. Washington had a better idea that was much more aggressive: take the working women to the British. In order to do this he would need the one thing that he had plenty of – camps full of women. With so much devastation taking place on the battlefields, camp followers regularly lost the men that they had followed to war. But this didn't mean that they no longer needed the protection or livelihood of the camps in order to survive. If anything, they were worse off than before.

Camp followers became increasingly valuable to the war effort as they were recruited into the espionage game. Already experienced as camp laundresses, cooks, etc., these ladies only needed to be trained in the proper methods of observation without detection, and how to note what was important and what was not. Throughout the war, destitute women whose properties had been confiscated were allowed to cross through sentry checkpoints to join family members caught behind either British or American lines in occupied cities or military encampments. Women who could offer services that were needed in the camps were welcomed with little hesitancy. Washington believed that he was killing two birds with one stone – thinning out the women in his camps, while gaining great amounts of badly needed intelligence.

Another perfect disguise for spies during the American Revolution was that of an elite, well-placed woman of society. Here again, this method of espionage required the enemy coming to the spy, but when large cities and towns, such as New York, Philadelphia, Charleston, or Savannah were occupied for substantial lengths of time, women of the upper class served both sides well. They could arrange, or easily be invited to, wonderful parties and balls that officers of occupying armies would certainly attend. At such events, conversations at the dinner table or on the dance floor were dominated by talk of the war. In this setting, rather than hoping to overhear juicy bits of important information, these women could manipulate conversations with cleverly directed questions or a sufficient stroke of an officer's ego.

On occasion these women not only had the ability to learn valuable information, but to manipulate events themselves. Mary Lindley Murray was a rebel sympathizer who was married to a wealthy Loyalist merchant and part-time royal official. The Murray's built a large homestead on 29 acres in present-day Manhattan Island, known as Inclenburg (now, Murray's Hill). With a commanding view of the British invasion of Manhattan at Kip's Bay, it took very little military understanding to realize that the lower portion of the island would be sealed off and General Israel Putnam's Americans trapped in New York City. With Putnam's army racing north up the post road along the Hudson River and the British advancing directly toward her property, Mary did the only thing that she could think of to buy the rebel retreat a little time – she stopped the British advance by inviting General Sir Henry Clinton and his officers to tea. Historians generally believe that Clinton was under orders to wait at Inclenburg for General Sir William Howe and the rest of the British forces to complete the landing, but it's well documented that "tea and cakes" were served – and we know how the British love their tea.

MAJOR JOHN ANDRÉ

Major John André has become known as Britain's spy master during the American Revolution. He recruited Benedict Arnold and convinced the traitorous American to reveal the plans for the fortress at West Point on the Hudson River in New York. Like Nathan Hale, André was caught red-handed (with the plans for the fort at West Point hidden in his boot!) and was dressed in civilian clothing. Unlike Hale, John André was the adjutant general to Sir Henry Clinton, supreme commander of all British troops in North America. André's execution brought charges of murder upon Washington directly from Clinton himself. Portrayed as a crafty, well-bred aristocrat who enjoyed playing the grand puppeteer, André didn't see himself in that light. In a letter to Washington on September 24, 1780, André confessed that he felt quite uncomfortable in the spy game because he was "too little accustomed to duplicity" to be any good at it. Of course, he was facing a hangman's noose and may well have said anything to escape the knot. Benedict Arnold would die angry, alone, and horribly unpopular, while John André is memorialized by a statue in Westminster Abby.

ROGUES'

Ann Bates was one of Britain's most effective spies during the American Revolution. Bates was a schoolteacher in Philadelphia and the wife of a British artillery sergeant. When the British evacuated Philadelphia in 1778, Mrs. Bates was left behind to basically fend for herself amongst the angry rebel sympathizers who had now come to power. But Ann was crafty and convinced all around her that she had secretly converted to the cause of independence and had vital information for General Washington. Ann was allowed to slip through rebel lines where, instead, she made her way to her husband's outfit. There he taught Ann everything she could learn about troop sizes, gun makes and types, cannon sizing, etc., and then helped her to find employment in Major John André's notorious spy ring. Once Ann had learned the ins-and-outs of military formations and what was important and what was not, the rest came naturally to her. Changing her last name to Barnes, Ann literally walked into Washington's camp at White Plains, NY, and listened in on campfire conversations and engaged officers in causal, but specifically directed, discussions about the war effort.

She was so adept at her deception that Major André sent her to several rebel camps and towns on many dangerous missions. If pretending to be a newly-arrived nurse, she could determine how many men the rebels could put on a battlefield by learning more about the number of wounded, injured, or sick in camp. As a cook, she could discover if the army was weak and grumbling from lack of proper food – and perhaps more importantly, where they were foraging for new sources of food. She also disguised herself as a vendor of various goods and products, giving her an excuse to remain in the area as long as she had something to sell without raising suspicion. Ann would later write that while in Washington's camp at White Plains she had opportunity to note things about the entire army, including details about each brigade, the number of cannon, their size, and how much powder for each field piece. Ann's career as a spy only ended once her husband's regiment had successfully taken Charleston in May 1780. She would join him there and eventually return to England in 1781, receiving a pension from the British government for her services.

PEGGY SHIPPEN ARNOLD

Peggy Shippen Arnold was the wife of America's most notorious traitor, Benedict Arnold. Though she herself was found innocent in her husband's treasonous plans, Peggy was forced to abandon her home and, eventually, her country. However, recent research tells us that Mrs. Arnold was definitely in on Arnold's scheme and helped to forward information between her husband and Major John André, with whom she had become acquainted when the British occupied her hometown of Philadelphia. Peggy's method for transmitting information was to encourage one of her girlfriends to write letters to André, which Peggy promised to pass on. While in possession of her friend's letter, the young spy would write information in invisible ink in-between the lines before sending it on.

NEW ORLEANS

Americans tend to think of the colonial history of New Orleans as basically one that "bobs" to the surface of the Mississippi delta just before Andrew Jackson arrived in 1815. But during the American Revolution, New Orleans was the capital of the vast Spanish territory of Louisiana. It was also the hub of Spanish and French efforts to aid the American rebellion prior to the entrance of those two empires into the war. In a nutshell, the espionage game in New Orleans centered around funneling military provisions and money to where ever the Continental army had needs.

It worked like this: working under the code name, Monsieur Hotalez, and a phony corporation, supplies were shipped from France either directly to the West Indies or first to Holland, where they were transferred to Dutch ships. Once in the Caribbean, the destination might be St. Eustatius, Martinique, or Haiti, before heading to Havana. British spies Robert Ross and John Campbell tell us that the cargo coming into Havana on French and Dutch ships were then transferred to Spanish ships before leaving for New Orleans. Another British spy, Alexander Graydon, notes that once in New Orleans, the cargoes were transferred to riverboats flying Spanish flags and crewed by Spanish and French sailors. The supplies were then rowed up the Mississippi where American riverboat men would receive the cargo at the junctions of either the Red or Arkansas rivers. They would then continue the grinding, upstream journey to Fort Pitt to be distributed.

Not all of the Revolutionary War espionage took place here in the colonies. Patience Wright was a noted sculptor of wax figures from Rhode Island, but a fire in her museum led her to take her skills to England where an artist could easily find wealthy patrons. While living and sculpting in London, the war in the colonies broke out putting Patience in a unique position. Adamantly faithful to her colonial homeland, she would discuss matters of state with her high-profile, very politically connected clientele while sculpting their images. Between what these people knew and what they overheard from their connections in London's aristocracy, Patience was able to gain information on British activities at the highest levels. And getting the information back to the colonies was quite simple, as New York was a British-held port throughout the war. Patience would hide messages in her wax figurines and images, then ship them to "interested clients" in New York. Today, her work can still be viewed in Westminster Abbey.

Patience Wright

Too many of the stories about these women have either been set aside for all the wrong reasons or perhaps are known only on a local basis. What happens that allows such remarkable accounts as these to be remanded to second-rate history? Perhaps that's why it's called history, because her-story is rarely told. But when it comes to the world of espionage, there are actually quite good explanations for such oversights, both for women and men. By now, many have learned of the Culper Ring of Setauket, Long Island, NY, and the vital role they played in Washington's need for information. We know that one of the key members of the ring was Anna Smith Strong, who was a vital link in the process for passing on key elements of intelligence gathered by this spy ring. However, another woman in the Culper Ring was deep undercover in New York City and is known only by her code name, Agent 355.

Anna's role in these events was discovered in 1939, when a collection of letters in her ancestral home was found. But the name and role of Agent 355 remains shrouded in mystery. The only facts we have at this writing is that Agent 355 was definitely a woman and, from the strength of the information she learned, her cover was that of someone well-placed in New York's elite society. That being said, this doesn't guarantee that she was the wife or daughter of a wealthy Loyalist. She may have been a servant in the home of such an individual or a trusted friend of the family. The other thing to remember about the identity of Agent 355 is that many spies in her circumstances only knew the people that they worked with directly. If neither Agent 355 nor her immediate contact survived the war, other members of the ring might never have been given the opportunity to meet her or learn her name.

Loyalists

Most Americans tend to compartmentalize the politics of the American Revolution into easily divided teams: redcoats/bluecoats; "Patriots"/"Loyalists"; Whigs/Tories; good guys/bad guys. But it just wasn't that simple. John Adams is credited with writing that 1/3 of the population of the British colonies favored rebellion, while another 1/3 were loyal to the Crown – and yet another 1/3 just wanted to be left alone. Loyalties to both political beliefs changed often and were heavily influenced by whichever army was occupying their pasture. Today we ask ourselves, "How could people have not been in favor of freedom?" But the question of freedom is heavily draped in the belief in the freedom to make personal and political decisions. Loyalists chose to remain dependent upon the current government, and that was their right. Thomas Brown was the great-grandson of Sir Isaac Newton and son of a wealthy shipping magnate. Brown was also a die-hard Loyalist and not shy about it. On August 2, 1775, approximately 100 Sons of Liberty from Augusta, GA, came to the home where Brown was staying and demanded he sign an oath of loyalty to the independence movement or face a severe beating. Brown scolded those who would claim to stand for liberty while demanding that he sacrifice his own freedom of choice in the process. Before the day was over, he would be beaten, scalped, tarred-and-feathered, and have hot brands put to his feet.

The East Florida Rangers

In December 1775, a fully recovered, seething Thomas Brown came to St. Augustine and was introduced to Governor Patrick Tonyn. Tonyn had built a small army of rugged backcountry Loyalist rangers, but he lacked a strong leader. Brown was his man. Brown was extremely intelligent, respected as an aristocrat, tough enough to handle the rigors of guerilla warfare, and very angry. The Rangers knew how to fight and how to survive in the country, but Brown taught them the art of espionage and the importance of gathering reliable information from rebel nerve-centers. He taught them the strategy and tactics of lightning-strike raids. Most importantly, he taught them to set aside their differences with the allied Native Americans and to utilize the skills they brought to this type of combat. General Augustine Prevost would incorporate the Rangers into the regular British army and rely upon Thomas Brown heavily in the campaign to re-claim Georgia in 1778.

A great many of the families who remained loyal ran five and six generations deep into the history of the American colonies. They simply couldn't understand how people could rise up in rebellion against the established form of government that they truly believed was ordained by God. In East Florida, the only British colony south of the Canadian border to remain wholly loyal throughout the course of the Revolution, assemblymen made declarations that it was their honor bound duty to *"recognize our allegiance to the blessed Prince on the throne, and the supremacy of Parliament; and be establishing on the most solid foundation, our constitution, liberties and dependence."*

THE FRANKLINS

Benjamin Franklin may well be one of the most famous people in American history. His daughter, Sarah Franklin Bache, was a staunch patriot and worked tirelessly in her efforts to support the war effort. George Washington writes to her in 1781, "Amidst the distress and sufferings of the Army, whatever sources they have arisen, it must be a consolation to our Virtuous Country Women that they have never been accused of withholding their most zealous efforts to support the cause we are engaged in." Franklin was equally proud of his son William, who had risen to the office of Governor of New Jersey prior to the war. However, as faithful as his sister was to her father's cause, William was just as faithful to king and country. When the old statesman couldn't sway his son to join the rebellion, Benjamin Franklin cut him off from the family and they never saw each other again. William's son, William, on the other hand, was at his grandfather's side at the Paris peace delegations that ended the war.

The war would destroy what was once a loving relationship between Ben Franklin and his son William.

Isn't it ironic that both Loyalists and their rebel adversaries believed in the exact same virtues for a sound government – a strong constitution (for Loyalists, the Magna Carta) that guaranteed certain liberties? For Loyalists, the sanctity of dependence, and having the right to choose to remain dependent, was just as virtuous as independence was to their counterparts.

The same issues in this study that

Sarah Franklin Bache: Crusader for Independe

faced women who favored independence also impacted the women who were Loyalists. But for these women, their first hurdle was to wrap their minds around the idea that something was wrong in the colonies. From these accounts we see a sense of confusion at times over what should be the right thing when it conflicted with what was actually taking place. For example, when fighting broke out in Lexington and Concord on April 19, 1775, no group of people where more shocked that issues had actually brought their colony to such dire circumstances than the Loyalists of Boston. Anne Hulton was the sister of Henry Hulton, the Commissioner of Customs in Boston – the man who levied taxes on all imports into New England. Anne's letter to a friend in England on April 22, 1775, speaks of the fighting in Concord and Lexington and reveals a great deal concerning a Loyalist's interpretation of what had taken place. Who was at fault? What were the

FOR KING AND COUNTRY

Women in support of independence, such as Rebecca Motte and her mother in South Carolina, weren't the only ones burning down their homes. Mrs. Patrick Tonyn, wife of the royal governor of East Florida, watched as her 20,000 acre plantation, two large manor houses, four mills, slave quarters, and all of the valuable crops - in short, the Tonyn's entire fortune - was burned to the ground in the spring of 1777. The governor had been informed that an invading rebel army was nearing his property and would likely provision itself off of his land and its vast resources. Being a military veteran of 33 years, Tonyn wouldn't allow such a thing to happen and set fire to all that he had. After watching their property destroyed, Mrs. Tonyn and her four children joined the governor in St. Augustine where they lived in one of the large town-homes of Lt. Governor John Moultrie, from 1777 until the evacuation of the colony in 1785. As fate would have it, the invading rebel army came no closer than sixty miles of the Tonyn's plantation - it was destroyed for nothing.

circumstances in Boston over next few days? One might expect that she would claim that the men of Massachusetts fired first, as most British reports stated. Or, perhaps, she would ridicule the manner in which the men of each town fired at the retreating British army from behind stone walls and then ran away. Instead, she writes of the tremendous fear that she felt when she first heard that the rebels had formed an army of 20,000 fighting men and surrounded Boston with cannons on every hill. You can feel a sense of shame when she states that British general Hugh Percy was refusing to let any more rebel sympathizers, or anyone else for that matter, leave Boston. Percy was using the people of Boston "as the greatest security; the general declared that if a gun is fired [into] the town, the inhabitants shall fall a sacrifice." And yet, understanding that she herself was one of those unarmed townspeople that General Percy declared to be expendable, Anne then writes about how grateful she was that Percy's life was spared in the fighting and how bravely and nobly he conducted himself. Anne Hulton was not an ignorant person and she had to wonder at the conflicting remarks that she made, even as she was writing them. Like so many others, Anne would dutifully return to England before the end of 1775 and never return.

A SAD CASE OF MISTAKEN IDENTITY

On September 12, 1775, General Thomas Gage ordered the Superintendent of the Southern Indian District to utilize the region's Native Americans to "...take arms against His Majesty's enemies and to distress them in all their power for no terms is now to be kept with them." Colonists in both the Northern and Southern Indian Districts were shocked by this edict because now every Loyalist and fence-straddler was in danger as well; many joined the rebellion. Native tribes rarely knew what settlers were on which side, especially with settlers changing sides so often! The story of one girl, Jane McRea, brought outrage against this edict from both sides. Jane was a young Loyalist who was left stranded when her fiancé enlisted to fight for a British militia in New York. While traveling to join him at his camp, Jane was killed by Iroquois warriors allied to the British.

This sensationalized image of the death of Jane McRae was used to stir up anger toward the British

SIEGE OF BOSTON

April 1775 - March 17, 1776

After the humiliating retreat of British troops from Lexington and Concord, resistance to imperial forces grew stronger by the day. On the map (left) the location of the Battle of Bunker/Breeds Hill (A) can be seen across the river to the North, just behind Charles Town. Even though the men of Massachusetts lost that battle, British casualties in the field were so staggering that it became a moral victory for the colonial militia. Notice the "neck" leading into Boston - the only way in or out by land (B). This narrow passage made it possible for colonial troops to seal the town. In January, 1776, 60 tons of artillery were placed on Dorchester Heights (C). The British had no option other than surrender. On March 17, 1776, the British evacuated Boston for good.

Not all Loyalist women could leave the continent once the war started. For many, this was their home. Living in the American colonies was the only life they had known and they either had no desire leave or simply couldn't afford to resettle on some distant shore. Benjamin and Mary Almy and their children made their home in Newport, Rhode Island, as did Mary's mother. Their tale was not unique in the sense that many families were divided by their devotion to one side or the other, but for Mary it was particularly difficult as she remained loyal while Benjamin joined the rebel army. Yet, even with such a monumental division in the home, letters back and forth show that the couple remained very much in love. Matters would grow worse from 1776 to 1778, as rebel troops had been held at bay by the British occupiers of Newport. On August 3, 1778, Mary's letters to Benjamin tell of the fear that was gripping the city and how she was making plans to move her mother and children to a safer location. But Newport is on an island and to leave was not so easily done. By August 6, Mary tells how the inhabitants have little choice but to drive cattle and other livestock into the protected perimeter of the British defenses and hope for the best. French bombardments began that day, increasing on the next. With the horror of a siege flying all around her, Mary managed to get her mother and children to safety on August 8, but she remained behind to help however she could. The British set fire to 16 buildings to deprive French troops of proper locations for hospitals, headquarters, and defenses. For the next three weeks the siege raged off and on, making sleep impossible – either due to the heavy bombardments or to the tension that mounted in-between attacks. On August 29, in what became known as the Battle of Rhode Island, British and Hessian troops cut down or injured about 500 rebel soldiers. Yet even after all that Mary and her family had been through, knowing that her husband was taking part in the siege that threatened their lives, Mary writes that she could only pray that Benjamin was safe, as rumors of British atrocities reached Newport. The siege failed and Newport would remain under British control until the area was evacuated in October 1779. As for Mary and Benjamin – they were reunited after the war and lived a long, happy life together. The heart wants what the heart wants.

Prudence I.
Dyres. I.
Goggershall P.te
Redwoods
Island.
Chemin de l'Ouest.
Chemin de l'Est.
Arnold's P.te
Almeys hill
Turkey hill
Denfey's hill
Butt's hill
Quakers hill
Premiere
Basfonds dont parties a Sec dans les Grandes Marées
Hog I.
Popasquash P.te
Ferry de Bristol.
Sandy P.te
Black P.te
Bridge
Hon. Thurmans P.te
Quay
Pocasset River
Howlands Ferry.
l'Est
Goulds I.
Vantons Cove
Tiverton.
Ouacut Pond
Wantons
Bridge

IROQUOIS CONFEDERACY

At the time of the American Revolution the Iroquois confederacy consisted of six powerful allied Indian nations whose lands spread across upstate and most of western New York. The league consisted of the Mohawk, Oneida, Onondaga, Cayuga, Seneca, and Tuscarora tribes. The Six Nations were bound politically by what was known as "The Great Law of Peace." During the Revolution the Iroquois Confederacy tried to remain neutral in hopes that the "English" and the "Virginians" would leave them in peace. But the war flooded onto their lands and split the nations. Only the Oneida and many of the Tuscarora allied with the Americans. Washington employed a harsh, destructive war on the other four nations, especially the Mohawk, destroying the effectiveness of the British/Iroquois alliance for the rest of the war. A Native American War of Independence was just beginning.

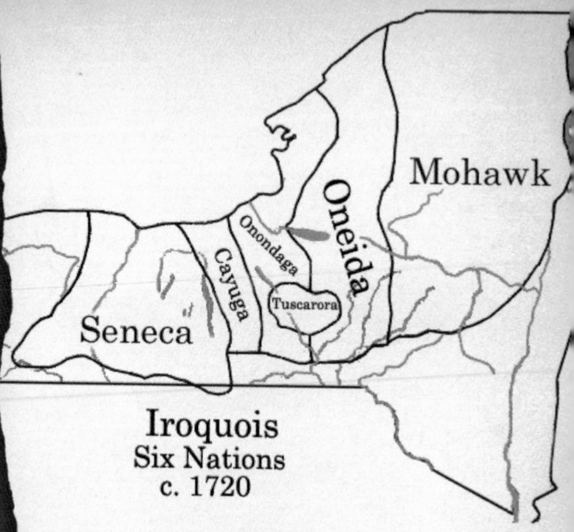

Throughout the summer of 1775, the southern colonies fell in domino-fashion to the rebellion. Southern Loyalists and their slaves flooded south in an effort to stay one step ahead of the American onslaught. Thousands journeyed as far south and west as the Loyalist safe havens of East and West Florida. Here they could begin a new life under the protection of the Crown. Many saw the Floridas as only temporary shelter that was close enough to their homes across the South to be easily accessible once the war ended. At the Special Collections Library at the University of Florida there can be found an original memoir of one such lady named Mary Port Macklin. Mary and her husband John owned a perfume shop in Portsmouth, England before coming to Charleston in 1774. There they salvaged the abandoned, derelict schooner, *Charlotte*, dragged it to the most popular pier in Charleston, and converted it into a popular "beef steak club" restaurant. Soon their "floating eatery" was a hit. They would later open The London Coffee House on Elliott Street, near the Charleston Exchange. Life was good!

But not for long. Once the rebellion had gripped Charleston, the Macklins were immediately under suspicion as John twice

The bustling harbor of Charles Town was the busiest and most profitable in the southern colonies

refused to sign loyalty oaths to the rebel government. By 1778, John had been jailed twice – the second time for 8 months and Mary along with him. Upon their release, John headed for St. Augustine, leaving Mary in Charleston, but he would soon return...as a prisoner of war. The Macklins would eventually escape and make their way back to St. Augustine. Sadly, Mary became so ill that she couldn't walk due to extreme pain in her limbs – yet John took to the sea once more, regardless. The house in St. Augustine that he claimed to have purchased for his wife was soon inhabited by other people who kept Mary confined to her bedroom. Before long, a kind family in St. Augustine took-in the sick and impoverished Mary, but her life was in ruins. Before the war the Macklins owned thriving restaurants that were frequented monthly by the governor of the colony. Now, a feeble Mary Port Macklin would serve her new family as a governess – never to see John again.

Not every Native American felt forced to join one side or the other during the American Revolution. Singing Bird, or Molly Ockett, as she became known, was an itinerant Abenaki healing woman. Though she spent much of her life in or near the White Mountains-region of what is now Maine, Molly could also be found walking hundreds of miles through New Hampshire and Vermont providing care for anyone in need

The Sea Islands of South Carolina and Georgia became home to former slaves who had found their freedom by running to these hard-to-reach regions of the swampy coasts. Here, they simply wanted to be left in peace as free people. Known as Gullah/Geetchee, these people have sought to maintain their anonymity and unique cultural blending of ancient African and African-American customs and traditions unlike those found anywhere else.

Flora MacDonald was perhaps the most famous of the Loyalist women in her day. From 1745-1746, the Scottish Jacobite Rebellion threatened to place the Catholic prince Charles Edward Stuart on the throne of Great Britain. When "Bonnie Prince Charlie" and his Scottish Highland army was defeated at the Battle of Culloden in 1746, Flora MacDonald accepted the task of sneaking the prince out of Britain and on to France.

She disguised Charles as a woman and successfully secured his safe passage. But Flora was caught and imprisoned in the Tower of London. After her release she was hailed a hero by the Highland folk and would later marry Allen MacDonald. In 1774, the MacDonald's sought a new life across the Atlantic. But rebellion was brewing steadily in the Americas, so the famous Jacobite and her family were pressed to sign an oath of loyalty to the Crown before leaving Scotland. They took their oath very seriously and settled in North Carolina, wholly loyal to King George III. In 1776, when the deposed royal governor of North Carolina called for militia to help reclaim his fallen colony, Allen MacDonald accepted the rank of major in the 84th Regiment of Foot (Royal Highland Emigrants). The regiment was called upon to march from present-day Fayetteville, NC, to meet a British invasion fleet at the Cape Fear River. The night before they marched, folks tell that Flora MacDonald gave the men a stirring speech that called for courage, honor, and loyalty to the Crown. The Highlanders rallied around this spitfire of a woman, but were soundly defeated at Moore's Creek Bridge on February 27, 1776. Flora's husband, son, and son-in-law, and many others of the 1,600 Loyalists were taken prisoner. The new government would not be as kind to Flora as were the British after Culloden in 1746. All of the MacDonald's properties were confiscated and Flora, finally reunited with her husband after years of separation, returned to Scotland penniless in 1779. Being a heroine for the losing side did not pay-off for Flora MacDonald a second time.

BATTLE OF MOORE'S CREEK BRIDGE

On October 16, 1775, King George III authorized a full-scale invasion of the southern colonies, which he dubbed "The Southern Expedition." One of the elements of this invasion that had been guaranteed was a 10,000-man Loyalist army from North Carolina. But Governor Josiah Martin's 10,000-man guarantee was in reality only 1,600 men who were in need of arms and ammunition. On their march to the Cape Fear River to meet the British fleet, the North Carolina Loyalists were intercepted at Moore's Creek Bridge by a smaller, but heavily armed, rebel militia. Only recently have we learned the full extent of the invasion that was designed to take place in March 1776, which brings the Battle of Moore's Creek Bridge into a much larger perspective in the War for Independence in the southern colonies.

Women in every colony faced the threat of abandonment as many of their Loyalist husbands chose the safety and comforts of England. Rarely did these ladies' stories turn out well, even for those whose refusal to join the rebellion was based on religious beliefs. Sally Wister and Anna Rawle were born into prominent Quaker families in Philadelphia and spent much of the war in the comfort of their family homes and mansions. Sally's journal of letters discusses her thoughts on the events that brought her family from their home in Philadelphia sometime in late 1776 or early 1777, to the safety of a family homestead in Germantown. For the next two years the sixteen-year old reports her perspective on Continental Army officers, several battles, the reoccupation and evacuation of Philadelphia by the British army, and dreams of returning to her home some day.

SALLY WISTER'S JOURNAL

A True Narrative

BEING A QUAKER MAIDEN'S ACCOUNT OF HER EXPERIENCES WITH OFFICERS OF THE CONTINENTAL ARMY, 1777-1778

EDITED BY
ALBERT COOK MYERS

WITH REPRODUCTIONS OF PORTRAITS, MANUSCRIPTS, RELICS AND VIEWS

FERRIS & LEACH · PUBLISHERS
Nos. 29-31 North Seventh Street, Philadelphia

An 1892 publication of Anna Rawle's journal leaves little doubt that a move out of Philadelphia may have been best. Often labeled as Loyalists, the Rawles most likely were simply neutral throughout the war. Either way, this was a time when neutrality could be just as offensive as taking sides. Once the British evacuated Philadelphia in 1778, those who believed in independence became bolder in their attitudes toward Loyalists and pacifists. Anna's world came crashing down on October 21, 1781, when news of Lord Cornwallis's surrender at Yorktown reached Philadelphia. Anna's journal is filled with frightening passages about mob violence, vandalism, lootings, home destruction, and beatings. On October 26, after six days of violence, Anna writes "It seems universally agreed that Phyladelphia [sic] will no longer be that happy asylum for Quakers that it once was. Those joyful days when all was prosperity and peace are gone, never to return; and perhaps it is as necessary for our [Quaker] society to ask for terms as it was for Cornwallis."

But few, if any, in Philadelphia felt the crushing blow of defeat like Grace Galloway. Grace was not only extremely wealthy in her own right, but married into a financial fortune, as well. Her husband,

Loyalist John Malcom of Boston on his way to be tarred-and-feathered

Joseph Galloway, had been Benjamin Franklin's political colleague since 1754, Speaker of the Pennsylvania Assembly, a member of the First Continental Congress, and was one of the wealthiest men in this region. But when Galloway turned his back on Franklin and the independence movement he became arguably the most despised man in Pennsylvania. Late in 1776, when he could no longer remain in Philadelphia, Galloway abandoned Grace and fled to British headquarters in New York. Her "job" was to protect their property from vandalism and remain in close contact with others in order to maintain their social standing. Theirs was never a marriage based upon happiness or love. Grace wrote openly concerning her marriage, stating that she was "neglected, loathed, and despised." But she was brought up in a stern culture that insisted wives be dutiful and obedient. She would do her duty. Galloway returned in 1777 with the British army, but abandoned Grace once again when the British returned to New York in 1778 – this time taking their only surviving child, Betsy. Galloway had made himself even more obnoxious to the people of Philadelphia during his brief return, making the protection of their property impossible once he left. All of their lands and homes were confiscated, with only the promise of having the land that Grace had inherited from her father be passed on to Betsy, but only after her husband was dead. For the next four years Grace lived with a Quaker woman and, though scorned publically by former friends and left to her own devices for money, she complained to no one. We only know of her struggles from the diaries that she kept from 1778 to 1779. Her husband, on the other hand, was granted a pension by the British government and received compensation for their lost lands. He sent Grace nothing but a few letters during this time. Galloway was never allowed to return to Philadelphia and Grace either could not or would not leave for England until her husband sent for her. He never did. Grace died a broken woman on February 6, 1782.

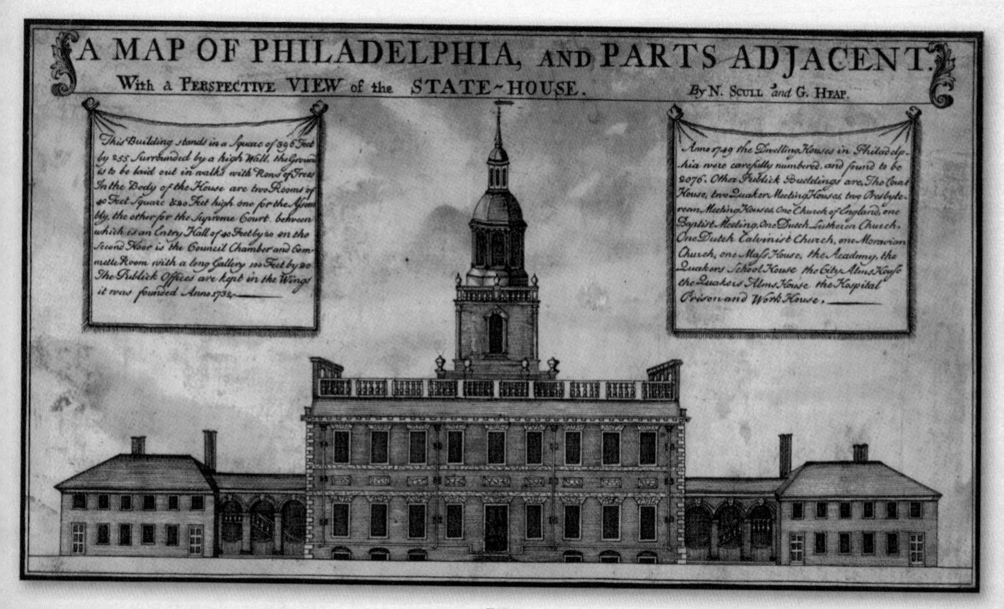

Women of the Pen

Most would argue that the collection of letters written by Abigail Adams to her husband and friends, particularly Mercy Otis Warren, are the most famous and popular of women's texts from the Revolutionary era. From these writings we can see that her great passion – second only, perhaps, her to family – was that of a quality education for young women. But it was much more involved than just the simple idea of what's good for the boys is good for the girls. The dragon she hoped to slay was the notion that girls need only to learn the proper procedures for running a home because that was what they were going to do...and nothing more. Boys, on the other hand, could be politicians, generals, ministers, lawyers, physicians, prominent planters, businessmen – the options were endless. Therefore, boys required an education in such things as the Greek classics and to read Latin; to understand the world's great philosophers and scientific advancements of the day. It was believed that the point behind the education of boys was to stimulate their minds to prepare them for the intrigues of whatever careers they ultimately chose. Other boys may not have had such options but they would become apprentices who learned trades with the potential for opportunities to raise themselves to higher levels of society. The best example of such a career path leading to wealth and fame would be Benjamin Franklin.

Mercy Otis Warren

Even before the American Revolution, Mercy Otis Warren wrote essays, poems, and even stage productions that mocked British dignitaries and their concept of governing the colonies - one play being titled "The Blockheads." While this might seem like a fashionable way to express political opinions today, Mercy was in danger of arrest for her writings, for no one was allowed such open expressions of dissatisfaction against the Crown, It wasn't difficult for Mercy to escape suspicion, however, as women weren't considered to be deep-thinking enough to form such opinions and in quite so articulate a manner. Mercy would go on to write the first history of the struggle for independence, but her account was slanted with her personal frustrations and criticisms for the lack of inclusion of women's rights in the overall outcome. John Adams was especially resentful of Mercy's work and some believe that it wasn't published until 1805 due the fact that she was a woman.

Abigail Adams

REBECCA PROTTEN

Not all of the women's stories from the Revolutionary era that demand to be heard come from war-related efforts. In his book, *Rebecca's Revival*, historian Jon Sensbach tells the story of a slave woman on St. Thomas, in what was then the Danish Virgin Islands. Rebecca Protten not only gained her freedom, but she became a Moravian evangelist in a day and age when slaves were severely discouraged, even forbidden, from hearing the teachings of Christianity, much less preaching them. Slave revolts of the late-18th and early-19th centuries found a good part of their stimulation in the teachings of Christianity - freedom through salvation. If Jesus could set their souls free from the shackles of sin, then why not their bodies as well? Rebecca's tireless determination to carry her ministry throughout the island of St. Thomas, regardless of personal harm, brought to her the attention of church leadership in Germany. Before her life ended in 1780, the ministry of Rebecca Protten would touch the hearts and souls of blacks and whites alike on three continents.

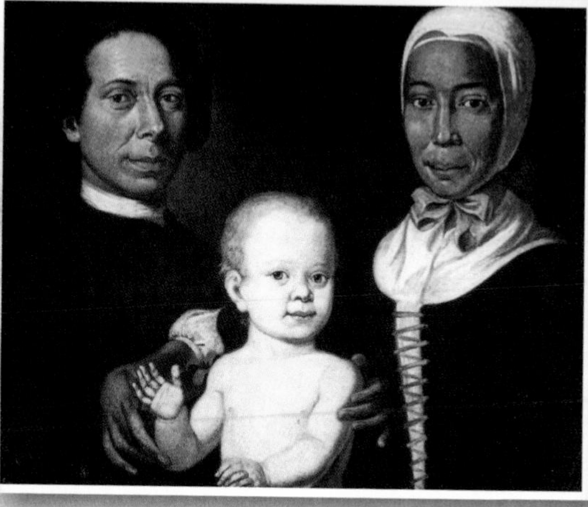

But Abigail Adams would write, "If we mean to have heroes, statesmen and philosophers, we should have learned women." On this, her husband agreed and answers, "In reading history you will generally observe, when you light upon a great character, whether a general, a statesman, or philosopher, [there is] some female about him either in the character of a mother, wife, or sister who has knowledge and ambition above the ordinary level of women..." (perhaps this is where we get the saying "Behind every great man is a woman"). Even with this statement of agreement, however, "the ordinary level of women" seemed to be quite low in John Adams's vision for the new nation.

The idea of educating girls beyond their obvious calling was considered frivolous to even the most intelligent men of this age. Thomas Jefferson, of all people, didn't favor equality in education for women, while promoting the idea that the only role a woman should play in politics was to be supportive of their husbands' political endeavors. Ironically (perhaps selfishly would be a better word), Jefferson made sure that his own daughter Martha received an excellent classical education. Jefferson hired tutors for Martha and established a regimen of reading and study that he would confess was stiff for a young girl in this country. But his reasoning was classic Jefferson: he considered that one day she would be "the head of a little family of her own. The chance that in that marriage she will draw a blockhead I calculate at about fourteen to one." While not giving his daughter much hope for attracting a bright-minded husband, notice how Jefferson refers to Martha's future position as "the head" of her family. This isn't an accident or slip of the tongue, but rather it's quite consistent with the concept that men of this era held dear the notion that women were responsible for the workings of the home and of the care of the family. This was their domain and he and the other founding fathers were determined to keep the status quo.

The great women writers of this era forged the earliest beginnings of the women's movements of the 19th and 20th centuries and received very little credit for the role they played. They did not protest; they weren't arrested, beaten, and jailed or publically humiliated, but they took those difficult first steps with their writings. In perhaps her most famous letter to her husband, dated March 31, 1776, Abigail Adams questioned the ethics of the southern colonies for holding slaves while screaming for liberty, among other insightful thoughts. But the line

Hope of Freedom

most remembered is when she reminded John to *"remember the ladies, and be more favorable to them than your ancestors. Do not put such unlimited power into the hands of the husbands. Remember all men would be tyrants if they could. If particular care and attention is not paid to the ladies we are determined to foment a rebellion, and will not hold ourselves bound by any laws in which we have no voice or representation."* Mrs. Adams makes it quite obvious that the founding fathers weren't the only ones aggravated to the point of revolt at having no representation! But her stern warnings were brushed aside more easily than even she thought possible.

CATHERINE MACAULAY

Not all of the great female writers of this generation who were sympathetic to the cause of independence were colonists. Catherine Macaulay had the rare luxury of a private education in Britain that was in line with that of her male counterparts. As a young woman Macaulay became a noted historian and tackled such topics as Parliamentarianism (do we really need a monarch?) and exposed Oliver Cromwell as a tyrant in her eight volume set *History of England from the Accession of James I to That of the Brunswick Line*. Though her republican sympathies created a great deal of controversy, Macaulay's work was highly respected and widely read by such women as Abigail Adams and Mercy Otis Warren, to whom she became a mentor.

By 1775, Macaulay's focus had turned to the issues in North America. She discussed the question of colonial taxation when she wrote "Address to the People of England, Scotland, and Ireland" in 1775. In 1777, she was introduced to Benjamin Franklin while in Paris and would be the guest of George and Martha Washington at their home after the war (though Martha would write that Macaulay's leaving made "happy those whom she left"). Martha had the grace and style to leave many of her opinions unspoken, but rarely unwritten!

No woman, rose further to be recognized as a great writer of her generation than a slave girl, Phillis Wheatley Phillis was born in Africa and approximately seven years old in 1761 when she was kidnapped by slaver hunters and shipped to Boston on the infamous *Middle Passage*. There, the child was purchased by the Wheatley family, who were insensitive enough to name her after the slave ship *Phillis* that brought her to them.

The Wheatley's 18-year old daughter, Mary, took it upon herself to teach Phillis how to read and write, but in less than two years the student was exceeding the teacher. By the age of 12, Phillis was learning Latin and English literature, particularly the challenging poetry of Alexander Pope. As thrilled as the Wheatley's were with Phillis's obvious genius, she was never considered to be anything more than a slave to them and treated more like a clever parlor exhibit to impress visitors. At the age of 20, and fighting life-long health issues, the Wheatley's sent Phillis to England, accompanied by their son Nathaniel. It's been questionable as to whether this trip was for her health, as the Wheatley's claimed, or were they sending their prize possession on tour. But we do know that Phillis had an English patron by the name of Lady Huntington, who found the young woman intriguing and paid well for her poetry.

It wasn't as though Phillis was ignorant of her circumstances. She was removed from the other slaves owned by the Wheatleys and treated "differently," but she was still a slave. She once wrote, "...in every human Breast, God has implanted a Principle, which we call love of Freedom; it is impatient of oppression, and pants for Deliverance – and by the Leave of our modern Egyptians I will assert that the same principle lives in us." Everything changed in 1774, when Mrs. Wheatley died. Phillis was granted her freedom, as a result, but her poetry would never find another patron. Phillis embraced the doctrine of liberty being shouted from the rooftops and wrote one of her most memorable poems about George Washington. Her poetry became an inspiration for other black artists of her day, such as the artist Scipio Moorehead and writer Jupiter Hammon. In fact, the only surviving piece of Moorhead's art work is his portrait of Phillis. Poverty and a never-ending battle with poor health was a bad combination in the 18th century. Phillis Wheatley died at the age of 31 – but she died a free woman.

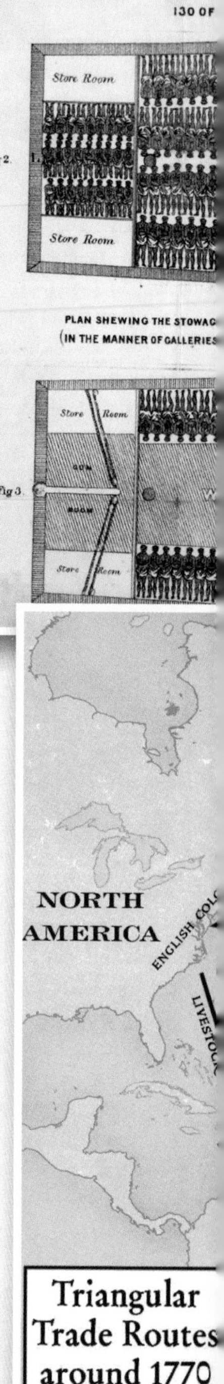

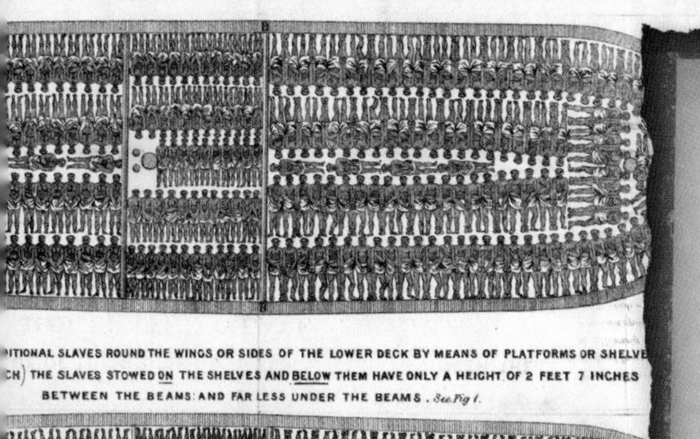

THE MIDDLE PASSAGE

The Middle Passage is a reference to the second stage of the colonial-era "Triangular Trade." In its most simple terms, 1) New England rum and other goods were traded to African kings in return for captured human beings; 2) the captured people were brought from Africa to the Caribbean by ship; 3) Caribbean molasses was shipped to New England to be distilled into rum (this, of course, is just one of the many facets of the slave trade and Atlantic World trade routes). The process of breaking a person's will and spirit so that they would become productive slaves took place during the long and cruel journey across the Atlantic Ocean. In his book, *The Slave Ship*, historian Marcus Rediker equates the Middle Passage to a factory that takes a raw, natural product (a human being from Africa) and, like a factory, manufactures that "product" into something completely different – a slave. Rediker believes that as many as 12.4 million Africans endured the Middle Passage. The U.S. outlawed the importation of slaves from Africa in 1808, though slavery itself was not abolished until the passage of the 13th Amendment in 1865.

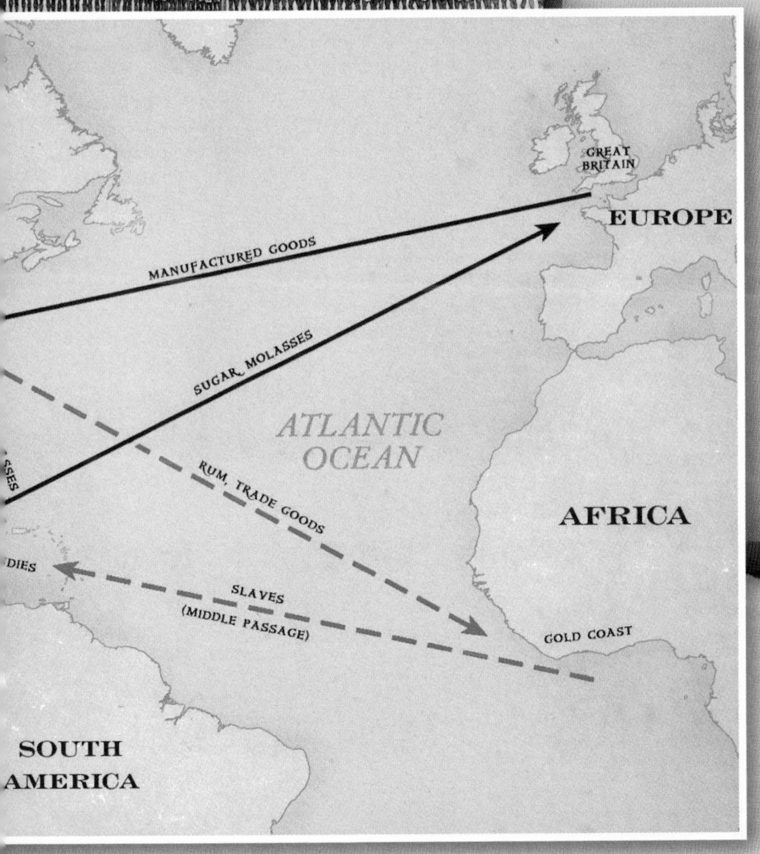

"Historians now estimate that 10 to 12 million Africans experienced the horrors of the Middle Passage

Annis Stockton was a renowned poet, chronicler of the American Revolution, and the wife of Richard Stockton, who signed the Declaration of Independence – as did her son-in-law, Dr. Benjamin Rush. When the British rampaged New Jersey, the Stockton's were forced to leave their estate near Princeton since Richard's prominent stance for independence made him a marked man. While trying desperately to avoid the British army, Annis took the time to save valuable papers of state, as well as the papers of the American Whig Society of Princeton College, by burying them in a safe place. But in doing so, she had no time to save her own writings and poems, all of which were destroyed when British soldiers ransacked their home.

Richard Stockton would spend most of the American Revolution suffering immeasurable atrocities in British prisons. He died on February 28, 1781, never realizing the final victory for which he sacrificed so much. Annis kept the family together and ran the estate, though virtually penniless. Through all of this, she continued to write, becoming one of the most highly acclaimed female authors of the 18th century.

GREAT SUCCESS... BUT AT WHAT COST?

Eliza Pinckney of South Carolina is praised for being one of the most remarkable women of the colonial era. Pinckney is said by many to have singlehandedly brought South Carolina into the global market of indigo production. But the process for turning an indigo plant into a cash crop was extremely labor intensive and created disease-ridden conditions for those who physically worked at the site. Pinckney writes of the horrific smell generated as the plant rotted, putrefied, and fermented in vats, producing noxious and poisonous fumes. She remarks that the smell was so intolerable that the factory must be staged a quarter mile or more from any dwellings on the plantation. She even noted that it was almost impossible to keep livestock on or near the area. Yet, enslaved human beings worked these manufacturing sites, by hand, daily. Yes, the success of Pinckney's efforts in indigo production brought tremendous wealth to the colony. In 1754, royal governor James Glen wrote that "negroes are sold at higher prices here than in any part of the King's dominions...a proof that this province is in a flourishing condition... I presume 'tis indigo that puts all in such high spirits." And what was the purpose of this valuable crop that the world seemed to depend upon so heavily that human lives were sacrificed to produce its fruits? Blue fabric dye. Wow...

Abigail Adams was not alone is her fight for equal education. Judith Sargent Murray, who is considered by many to be the founder of the American feminist movement, took notice of the inequalities in education when her younger brother was allowed a superior education to her own, simply because he was male.

Judith Sargent Murray

Murray would find her loophole when she and her entire family converted to Universalism, the belief that everyone is capable of receiving eternal redemption on the basis that all people are equal. If she was equal to her brother when it came to eternal redemption, certainly she should be considered his equal in the classroom. Her most famous essay, "On the Equality of the Sexes," was actually written in 1779, though it wasn't published until 1790 due to its feminist tone. Murray taught here that "genius" is the result of study, not gender, and that the scholastic tragedy of gender/educational inequality is that men were convinced that women were incapable of a comprehending a classical education. But then the men would mock women when that very lack of educational opportunity kept ladies from discussing the more complicated topics of the day. In short, Murray preached, don't deprive me of an education and then treat me like I'm inferior because I'm uneducated! Murray would defend the intelligence of women as a whole by discussing how they have proven, through what little opportunity they have had, their powers of logic, ingenuity, and creativity within the boundaries that society has allowed them. Imagine, she asks, what women could accomplish if they were offered an equal education and how all would benefit if the population of educated, free-thinking minds were doubled.

MARY WOLLSTONECRAFT

Mary Wollstonecraft is often considered one of the greatest women writers of the Revolutionary era. The fact is, she didn't publish her first pamphlet, "Thoughts on the Education of Daughters" - considered by many to be her finest work - until 1787. While that doesn't lessen her impact on feminine issues in early American history, it was the influence of earlier female writers that fueled her passions, not vice-versa. Mary Wollstonecraft may very well be the greatest example of someone taking up the torch and leading the next generation of women on those next difficult steps toward equality. Mary died in 1797, just 11 days after giving birth to her daughter, Mary Wollstonecraft Shelly, the author of *Frankenstein*.

CONCLUSION

When the dust had settled and the war had been won, the men who were running this new country grappled with the difficult growing-pains of changing from the loose-knit structures of the Articles of Confederation that had carried them through a revolution to a nation united under a constitutional government. The ladies would quickly realize that they had indeed been forgotten, as the men believed that such matters were trivial compared to the process of forging a nation. Forgotten were the leadership roles put upon the women by men, and the sacrifices made, in order that the Non-Consumption/ Non-Importantion boycotts might be extended to their maximum capacities. Forgotten were the political identities that women had formed of their own doing – even under the restrictions of the laws of Coverture that dictated otherwise – in order to support the political cause of their choosing. Forgotten was the courage displayed so many times throughout the war as women were left to determine their own fates (which, ironically, was something that they supposedly weren't capable of doing) in the face of danger from every direction. Whether by staying behind to face whatever consequences came their way or by following the armies – typically with several children in tow – the women of a young nation had proven themselves to be valiant and strong under every circumstance, over and over again. Gone were the opportunities for women to achieve the status of citizenship that they had envisioned for themselves and the women who were to follow in their footsteps for many generations to come. Gone...but not forgotten.

"*America* Guided by *Wisdom*"

America's 1st First Lady

Or, perhaps it might be better said that the women may have wished that they *had* been forgotten. For the solution to the question of "What to do with the ladies?" was resolved (at least, in the minds of the founding fathers) that young girls should be allowed a (somewhat) better education, but only for the purpose of raising their sons to be great leaders of the new republic. This was the birth of the concept that became known as "Republican Motherhood." This "new" status for women was little more than a sprucing-up of the same old rhetoric that the home was still the domain of women while very little outside of the home had changed in any way. This heralded new station for women was promoted under the banner that the Republican Mother had the single most important duty within the borders of the United States – to raise good, patriotic sons who would grow up to be the next generation of leaders. To do this, it was allowed that the education of young ladies might include more reading and writing, but nothing serious. Just enough to help their sons maintain a steady path toward leadership. The primary function of an extended education for girls was to insure that the homes of the Republican Mothers – a boy's first classroom, so to speak – would provide a positive influence for the lads, inspiring them as they prepared for their pre-ordained positions of political leadership and service to the country.

This was a far cry from what Abigail Adams envisioned for the future of young American women. One of her greatest objectives for a new nation with a fresh beginning was a complete reversal of the laws of Coverture and to obtain equal opportunities in education for young women, not just remedial reading and writing. An equal education to that of young men would bring many new opportunities: 1) if women could prove objectively – in a classroom setting – that they were capable of excelling in the very

The new republic's idea of family

same educational endeavors as men, then, 2) women could prove that they were capable of making intelligent decisions on equal terms with men, and, 3) if women could prove that they were capable of making the same intelligent/intellectual decisions as men, then women would be able to prove that they were intelligent enough to vote. And once women could gain the vote, then – and only then – would 50% of the nation's population have proper representation in government and, therefore, have an equal voice in the decisions that affect every individual on an every day basis.

While a country won its independence, the same cannot be said for its women. The ideals of Republican Motherhood would serve to keep women removed from the vote for almost 140 years. Enslaved African and African-American women had far greater concerns than the right to vote. Their primary concern was surviving to see the next day. Yet, as deplorable as their circumstances may have been, they had value to those who owned them. Even the cruelest of owners understood that a slave had to be alive in order to perform the tasks that they were purchased to perform. Sadly, even this most basic notion of economics could not save many of these women from fatal abuse. Perhaps Native American women held the least secure status of all in the post-revolutionary era. In the eyes of the new nation, these women served only one purpose and that was to produce more Native Americans – and Americans didn't want more Native Americans, they wanted their land. Therefore, the only real value of these women to the new nation was target practice. We had a very long way to go after the American Revolution...and we still do.